IGNITING THE BRAND

IGNITING THE BRAND

Strategies that have shot brands to success

JONATHAN CAHILL

Marshall Cavendish
Business

First published in 2008 by:

Marshall Cavendish Limited
Fifth Floor
32–38 Saffron Hill
London EC1N 8FH
United Kingdom
T: +44 (0)20 7421 8120
F: +44 (0)20 7421 8121
sales@marshallcavendish.co.uk
www.marshallcavendish.co.uk

A CIP record for this book is available from the British Library

ISBN-13: 978-1-904879-09-1
ISBN-10: 1-904879-09-8

Printed and bound in Great Britain by
TJ International Ltd, Padstow, Cornwall

CONTENTS

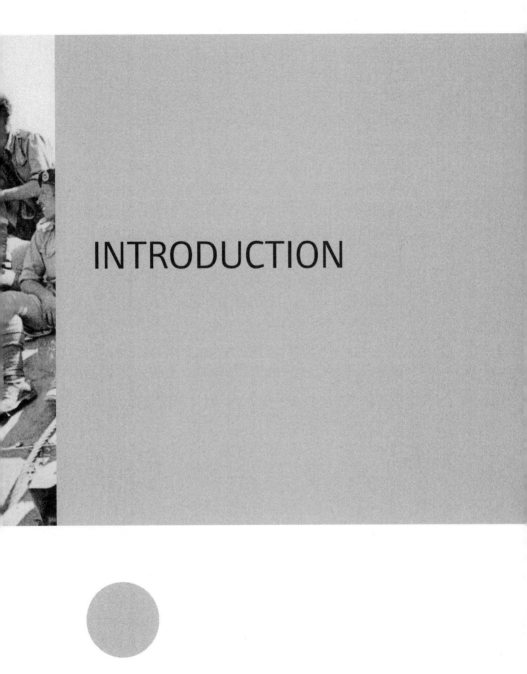

INTRODUCTION

"Brand" is a term that is currently having its day, sprayed with abandon on any commercial enterprise from Beck's beer to David Beckham, from Golf to Google. In most cases the work that has gone into achieving or maintaining this accolade has been assiduous. The most important aspect of such effort is deciding what is core to the marketing of the brand, the centre around which all activity should revolve – the strategy. Often it might appear a rather simple form of words. This should not obscure how much thought has gone into it. As in many things, the simple solution is often the best. This is particularly true of strategies, where, as they are essentially guides for people to follow, simplicity provides the bonus of a clear path and less room for confusion.

The strategy is the navigator for the brand. As with any journey, taking the wrong route can land you in trouble. Should your compass be true, then there's a better chance of arriving at your destination – marketing success. There is much theoretical work on strategy, but less based on real situations. As James March of Stanford University, one of the most highly regarded management writers in the USA, stated: "It is the combination of academic and experiential knowledge, not the substitution of one for the other, which yields improvement." This book is an attempt to balance the overwhelming weight of theoretical knowledge with some empirical data.

"The results of your campaign depend less on how we write your advertising than on how your product is positioned"
David Ogilvy

Usually, when case studies are cited, as in award schemes or books, the relationship between the marketing input and a successful outcome is often anecdotal and a coincidence is assumed to be a connection. It is deduced that what is achieved is due to what was put in. In terms of common sense, this usually seems likely, but when rigorously analysed the link is seldom proved. There is however one awards scheme where, in order for the case histories to win, there has to be a clear causal, as opposed to coincidental, link between input and success. This is the Advertising Effectiveness Awards, which have run in the UK for 27 years and have been extended to other countries. Through a rigorous factoring out of any other influences, they provide the assurance that the marketing success cited has a direct causal link to the strategy and its articulation in advertising. This book is the first time these winning strategies have been made readily accessible.

Some might question the use of cases from advertising to illustrate the marketing process, and it is true that however creative and appealing the advertising may be, it is of little use if it is pointing in the wrong direction. David Ogilvy, one of the most famous advertising figures of the twentieth century, listed 38 points for creating advertising that sells, and in first place he put "the most important decision", emphasizing that "the results of your campaign depend less on how we write your advertising than on how your product is positioned". In the cases featured here the advertising is simply an articulation of the strategy. There are exceptions, where the creativity of the advertising has transcended mundane strategies – these have been excluded from this book.

"The tools that can fashion a winning strategy are much simpler human traits: curiosity, common sense, a keen sense of context and a modicum of intelligence"

The most striking point to emerge from these cases is that there are no easy formulae. What distinguishes the winners is that the strategies used are not imposed on the brands, but rather grow out of them and their context. A good example of marketing that ignored this vital process was the dot-com crash. During this marketing frenzy the bold belief touted by those involved was that only the brand name needed to be communicated and not what it stood for. The result of such supposedly revolutionary thinking was a rather large bubble, which promptly burst.

To make a firm strategic leap, a deep understanding of the market, the brand and its interaction with consumers is needed. The strategic leap, like any other, has to be made from firm ground. This is provided by research, insight and intuition. To transform these into a meaningful strategy, many employ arcane rituals and incomprehensible jargon, rather like a French chef with an over-elaborate sauce. These are deployed with the same imperious confidence exemplified by those who caused the dot-com crash. The tools that can fashion a winning strategy are much simpler human traits: curiosity, common sense, a keen sense of context and a modicum of intelligence.

This may sound facile, and there is little doubt that the work that goes into achieving a winning strategy can be arduous. Like all great solutions, however, the cases in this book demonstrate that winning strategies often have a deceptive simplicity – which is where their beauty lies.

1

A JOURNEY OF 1,000 SHARE POINTS STARTS WITH THE PRODUCT

The key to any strategic success is the product and its relation with the consumer

The beginning and end of a product is that a consumer buys it to fulfil a largely functional need. What distinguishes a brand is that it meets an additional emotional need. This can be unearthed by examining the product, and more importantly by looking at the emotional relationship that can be fostered between the consumer and the product to help

---

"Branding is essentially taking the product on the journey from I–It to I–Thou"

---

transform it into a brand. The philosopher Martin Buber believed that man is born relational, and suggested that there were two main ways in which persons relate: with things, and with other persons. These he defined respectively as I–It and I–Thou relations. Branding is essentially taking the product on the journey from I–It to I–Thou.

MARKING OUT YOUR OWN PLAYING FIELD

Sometimes it is a question of juggling with the functional and the emotional, as in the case of Treasures Giggles disposable nappies in New Zealand. They were firmly in the mid-market sector and in three years had lost 10% in brand share. This was due to the absence of marketing support in this segment of the market and to fierce price competition with Huggies, who discounted up to 25% so that, although they were in the top sector of the market, their prices were close to Giggles. Also, the premium sector had improved the quality of their products by incorporating cloth-like breathable outers into the nappies, whereas Giggles stuck with plastic outers.

The challenge facing Giggles was to redefine their mid-market segment. A clear division was needed between this sector and the premium part of the market to ensure that Ultra, Treasures' premium brand, was not cannibalized, and also to take Huggies out of the value equation. In looking at consumers' attitudes it was realized that a more informed first-time or second-time mother realized that there were occasions when a premium nappy was not necessary. This was because they would change a nappy so many times a day that the superior performance of a premium brand was wasted. Consequently the cannier mothers would use a mid-market nappy during the day and a premium one at night, when its superior absorbency was required. Giggles' product performance, however, was considered inferior to that of most comparable products.

Faced with this situation Giggles hit on an ingenious "trickle down" approach in terms of the brand's performance. The premium brands were always trying to improve their product to maintain their position and justify their premium. This provided Giggles with the opportunity to pick up some crumbs from the premium table, by adopting previous innovations in the premium sector themselves and presenting them as something new in their sector. They upgraded the product with a cloth-like outer and slightly improved the absorbency. This enabled them to make the proposition to consumers: "Treasures Giggles has all the performance I need at the right price."

Not only was this working on the practical level of value, but it was also pandering to the consumer's self-image, as no nappy brand had ever treated the mid-market buyers as smart and deserving of a quality product. Having made these positive changes, Giggles placed greater emphasis on the brand's mid-market position, not by reducing the price of the nappies, but by reducing the average number of nappies per pack by just four. This was sufficient to allow a reduction in the pack price of 7–15%, although the actual price per single nappy rose slightly. Consequently Giggles were able to move the brand beyond the reach of the premium brands' predatory price cuts. Having fenced off this field for themselves, Giggles flourished, with volume market share rising 7.3% (from 28.2% to 35.5%) in the first month, and overtook Huggies as market leader. In addition their market penetration rose from 58% to 74%, extending their domain to many new buyers.

THE PRODUCT DOESN'T HAVE TO LEAP, JUST A SKIP WILL DO

The approach of Giggles was thorough and comprehensive. By contrast that of Fram SureGrip in the USA might appear purely cosmetic. It met a clear consumer need, however – always a good place to start. The market for oil filters purchased and fitted by consumers had stagnated and declined. The category was becoming a commodity business with price and promotion driving sales. Fram was losing out.

In light of this Fram got up close to the consumer and discovered that they viewed changing oil filters as frustrating: the oil on the filters could make them lose their grip, which might result in their hands being burned by the manifold or by dripping hot oil. To solve this problem they came up with Fram Extra Guard with SureGrip, which gave a rough, textured surface to the oil filter, providing consumers with a better grip. Fram's sales increased by 12.5% and their market share rose from 49.2% to 60%, all while sustaining a 10% increase in price.

Such a simple focus was also the approach of Huggies when they launched in the UK, which, in the context of their loss to Giggles in New Zealand, gives some feel for the swings and roundabouts of global brands. The UK market was dominated by Pampers, with a 77% share. They enjoyed particular advantages, not least that they had become the generic. Also their position gave them considerable distribution advantages, as supermarkets often used

Pampers for their own promotions. All this was against a background of low brand switching, as mothers were averse to risk where their babies were concerned.

Despite having such a dominant position Pampers were not complacent. They anticipated the launch of Huggies Ultrathins by introducing their own brand of thin nappies – Pampers Ultrathins. This appeared particularly problematic for Huggies as they were a one-product brand, and having Pampers make a sub-brand of the product they were launching risked pushing Huggies into a special-occasion niche.

In the face of this threat Huggies toughed it out and launched as a high-performance thin nappy. Emotionally they further differentiated Huggies by focusing less on the consumers' role as mothers and more on their children. They had a strategy of constant product improvement of the base product, rather than launching sub-brands as Pampers did, so it was their brand as a whole which was improving rather than aspects of it. In response, Pampers continued to launch new products, but in a diffuse way – at one time having five sub-brands. None of them had a significant effect on their overall share.

The simple but ingenious solutions employed by Giggles were also the basis of a less multifaceted approach adopted by Crown paint in the UK. It had an old-fashioned and declining brand share and wanted to position itself as a younger and more contemporary brand. To achieve some differentiation for the brand they took a tangential approach to the needs of someone painting at home and produced a paint with less odour. This they called "Breatheasy" in order to claim this new territory. Also they incorporated this feature in all their emulsion colours rather than creating a specific sub-brand. The only smell that lingered was the smell of success, with value share rising by 5.2 percentage points, worth £95.8 million.

IT'S THERE, STARING YOU IN THE FACE

Often the opportunity that the product presents is right in front of you, but it becomes apparent only when someone digs it up through assiduous research or, as in the case of Weet-Bix in Australia, it crops up by chance – in which case someone has to spot it. Things weren't looking good for Weet-Bix, as the relevance of its nutritional position was being undermined by parents submitting to increasing time pressure and so becoming more flexible about breakfast – letting their children eat more "treat" cereals rather than purely healthy ones. Weet-Bix had previously enjoyed success with a "low-sugar" position that focused on the brand's core nutritional values, and they wanted to keep this focus for the follow-up. Research suggested, however, that the low-sugar route would generate an adverse reaction among consumers who were buying Weet-Bix because of a belief in its overall nutritional value, not just because it was low in sugar.

It was at this point that chance intervened. A nutritionist working as a consultant for Weet-Bix's advertising agency on other business mentioned that he recommended it in his day-to-day work with clients seeking dietary advice. He thought others in his profession probably did so as well. This little marketing spark was then fanned by some research which involved sending out self-completion questionnaires to members of the Dieticians Association in New South Wales, who were involved in day-to-day dietary recommendations to clients. More than 90% of them said they recommended Weet-Bix for children, which led to the simple proposition that nine out of ten dieticians recommended the brand. This resulted in growth in market share from 9% to 11.3%, while that of major competitors Kellogg's Corn Flakes and Nutri-Grain fell from 9% and 8% to around 7.5%, marking the first significant share gap in three years.

Both Giggles and Crown created solutions to their situations, yet with Chicago Town Pizza in the UK the point of difference was already there. When it was launched there was no great loyalty to the existing brands, with most of them adopting an Italian angle. Consequently Chicago Town Pizza's position as the "authentic American pizza" was distinctive and was underwritten by its claim to be America's "best-selling frozen pizza". It soon became the best-selling one in the UK as well, and the American sector came to account for 50% of branded pizzas.

Although a lot of the success of this new sector had been due to Chicago Town, it now no longer had any strong differentiation from the other American pizzas that had followed on its coat-tails – a familiar problem in a market that one brand has initially created. To remedy this weakness, a new deep-dish pizza was developed that was smaller than other pizzas – being 13 centimetres in diameter as opposed to the normal 23 centimetres. Also it was the only one that could be cooked in an oven or a microwave and its deep-dish form was unique. This combination gave the brand a clear edge and the deep-dish pizza achieved the second-highest level of penetration in the market, with the regular Chicago Town Pizza holding top spot. Despite heavy discounting, the brand managed to maintain a premium that fuelled further investment and led to the company being transformed from a modest manufacturer of own-label pizzas into a firm with one of the UK's top 50 FMCG brands and the third-largest pizza manufacturer in Europe.

BACK TO THE FUTURE

The success of the Chicago Town Pizza brand stemmed from its roots in the USA, which weren't too difficult to spot. It was the foresight to use this as the main plank for the brand which made the difference. Often the past of a brand can provide a firm base for storytelling (one of the basic means of human communication) about the brand. As Gavin Fairburn, Professor of Ethics and Language at Leeds University, puts it: "Storytelling is central to most of human life. It is also the most startlingly simple and direct way I know of encouraging the development of empathy." Given the need for a brand to develop an emotional link with the consumer, its own story can be a compelling bond. It was

---

"**Storytelling is central to most** of human life. It is also the most startlingly simple and direct way I know of encouraging the development of empathy" Gavin Fairburn

---

looking to their past which gave Labatt's Alexander Keith's India Pale Ale in Canada a bright future.

Alexander Keith's had been brewed in Halifax, Nova Scotia, since 1820, and was the number-one beer in eastern Canada. There had been a change in the beer market, which gave an opportunity for the brand to expand out from its homeland. Mainstream beers were beginning to be seen as generic and consumers were attracted by beers that came from somewhere different or had a distinct story. The market began to fragment owing to the growing popularity of microbreweries, imports and speciality beers. History, craftsmanship and a distinct colour and taste became compelling stories, justifying a price premium. This seemed to present an open door to Alexander Keith, and the brand launched in Ontario with a position built on its Nova Scotia imagery. Unfortunately this did not have the desired results.

The brand had developed primarily as a draught beer and, as a result, the main consumers were in their late twenties and thirties, a group that consumed less than the younger guys. Consequently Labatt's decided to speak to slightly younger drinkers – aged 25 to 30 – who appreciated a more sophisticated beer. In talking to them, Labatt's homed in on the fact that speciality beer drinkers needed to feel proud of their choice of beer. They put more thought into selecting a beer, and the brand became a badge they were proud to display.

The heritage of Alexander Keith had all the elements required to meet this consumer need; it was just a question of how these attributes should be presented. They were distilled into a simple proposition: "Alexander Keith's is the pride of Nova Scotia. A pride worthy of respect." This built on the brand's brewing heritage, a rich history, and the legend centred on the brewmaster, Alexander Keith. It was further developed into the idea that there was a certain etiquette required in drinking the beer, playing to the attitudes that had been identified in the target group. And it benefited them in market share. A year and a half after the adoption of this position the brand's share had grown by 33% in Ontario and the west of Canada and it had become the number-one speciality beer in Canada.

Although Lee jeans in New Zealand could not call on such depth and history as were available to Alexander Keith, an appreciation of their provenance and past did give them an edge. They had nearly been abandoned by the all-important young jeans wearers. Retailers would look to Levi's as their mainstay and smaller, hipper brands to answer the fashion requirement. Lee had launched a new position based on the "New Look of Lee". This was liked, but was so different from the perceptions younger consumers had of Lee that they couldn't square the position with the brand and attributed it twice as often to Levi's as they did to Lee.

"A solid, functional base to which Lee's history added an emotional twist – cool"

Trying to scratch this rather dispiriting surface, Lee received confirmation that they were not seen as cool, but there was grudging respect for the durability of the jeans. The ideal jean was described as making the wearer feel so confident that they could do anything – as though they were indestructible. Lee's heritage contained a product that fitted this feeling like a glove – Lee dungarees, which had an indestructible spirit and had been around for 110 years. This was a solid, functional base to which Lee's history added an emotional twist – cool. The Buddy Lee Doll, a doll which was used as a promotional item from 1921 until 1962, was not known by the target audience, but was considered to be cool. Buddy and the man of action were combined with the line from the 1940s – "can't bust 'em". The effect in the market was hot; among the key 20 to 24-year-old target market, share increased from 2% to 20.6% in two years.

While Lee had trawled its heritage with success, Volkswagen went back to its emotional hinterland when it needed to adopt a winning position for its Polo model. Most small-car advertising focused on emotions or attitudes, positioning the cars as enablers of carefree fun. This common ground made these qualities appear generic and interchangeable, however. Consequently Polo went for something more solid which was true to the product and credible for the Volkswagen brand. They adopted the position of "built without compromise". This had the added benefit of making the well-known higher price of Polos more digestible for consumers, as the price then became a reason to believe in their superior quality. The improvement in the market share was equally solid, with monthly shares reaching historical peaks of 23.2 and 24.1%.

A BRAND TO LEAN ON

Just as Lee found an angle in the heritage of the product, so Swan Vesta matches in the UK found strength within their product. They were being badly beaten in the market by lighters, which were regarded not simply as a means of getting a light, but also as an item signalling social distinction. Matches were seen as the poor man's alternative.

Research revealed some important differences in perceptions. Matches were seen as natural, readily available and a traditional part of life which was reliable. In contrast, lighters, despite their superficial gloss, were regarded as expensive, easy to lose and liable to break down or run out of fuel or flint. Also, it was realized that it would be easier to persuade those who used matches as well as lighters – about 44% of smokers – rather than those who were using only lighters.

These insights resulted in the portrayal of lighters as the "unreliable light", whereas, with Swan, "it's nice to know something you can rely on". Although this message was simple it ignited sales, which rose by as much as 17% in one area. After a period of decline, matches consistently increased their share of lights.

The desire of the consumer to be able to rely on a brand also proved successful for Verizon Wireless in the USA. There was a price war in their market, but, after significant capital investment in their network, they couldn't afford price-driven competition.

In considering this conundrum they looked at the product and realized that the one consumer issue that no competitor was fully addressing was the basic requirement that the phones worked. Verizon set out to own reliability by stating that every day their employees drove all around the country to test the reliability of the network – with the claim "Verizon never stops working for you". In response they gained 723,000 new customers as compared with a target of 400,000.

ENSURING THE BRAND STARTS FROM THE RIGHT PLACE

Sometimes it's not a question of looking for something that's inherent within the brand or can underwrite what it offers; rather it's a question of making sure the product itself is given a strong start. The drinks company IDV in the UK felt they could capitalize on a trend from dark to light drinks and on the perception that dry drinks, which tended to be light or pale, were more sophisticated than sweet ones. In line with this they developed a product for the sherry market which had the preferred sweet taste and gave it a fashionable pale colour. Rather than make up a name, they chose to look for one with some provenance and found Croft. They had been established in 1648 as a port shipper, but had little contemporary presence. They called the brand Croft Original. This turned out to be firm ground for growth, with market share increasing from 3.6% to 10.7% within five years. Although the market began to lose users, Croft bucked this trend with continued advances.

A change such as that effected with Croft was slightly one-dimensional, whereas that wrought by Source yogurt in Canada was multifaceted. When it was launched, the diet yogurt market was identified as the strongest sector, with 25% growth. It was dominated by Silhouette, with a 94% share. The context in which the market operated was deceptive, however. Women turned out to be more health conscious and less calorie obsessed than had originally been thought. They wanted a more substantial health benefit than just fat- and sugar-free yogurt. Also they liked sweeteners, but not the aftertaste that came with so many of them.

These factors resulted in Source developing a product that had a taste that was preferred over that of Silhouette, and which also enjoyed a health advantage, thanks to the addition of calcium and vitamins A and D. The sweetness was provided by fructose and sucralose (Splenda), a sweetener with no aftertaste. On an emotional level the name Source was found to have echoes of purity, water and freshness, combining to give a clean and healthy image.

"On an emotional level the name Source was found to have echoes of purity, water and freshness, combining to give a clean and healthy image"

All these different facets were melded into positioning Source as a diet yogurt for health-conscious women in search of an underlying sense of well-being – a woman who cared more about feeling great rather than just looking that way. And care they did, as within one year Source's market share had reached 35% and the sector itself grew by 45%.

THE BRAND IS NOT JUST THE PRODUCT, BUT WHAT COMES WITH IT

The success of Source had been due to fine-tuning the product and its position in the light of the market context. With Carters Building Supplies in New Zealand the change in the product, in terms of the service offered, was more profound. Around 95% of its business was with the trade, which saw it primarily as a timber merchant. In addition the dominance of the trade meant that most of their range had become commoditized.

The rise in the popularity of DIY presented Carters with a big opportunity to widen their reach to consumer renovators and odd-jobbers. It was reasoned that they would be likely to respond to the added value in Carters' implicit expertise and so allow Carters to charge a premium price. Carters didn't want to alienate their trade customers, however. They wanted to encourage the associations with helpful advice and appear approachable, professional and knowledgeable. Carters had to be on the consumer's side, working alongside them, almost like their mate in the trade. This was expressed by the proposition "Carters – your building partner".

Adopting such a position fitted logically into their strategic approach. They needed to be able to deliver on this promise, however, and it was here that they changed their product in terms of the service provided. They introduced "Carters Consulting", which involved advisers on phones who could give immediate advice and ideas and could put the customer in touch with reputable tradesmen in their area – they were truly a "building partner". Certainly consumers seemed to think so, with sales increasing by 27.2% in a year and the proportion of turnover accounted for by non-trade customers rising from 5% to 12%.

GIVING THE BRAND LEGS

Pretty Polly tights (pantyhose) adopted a broader approach in the face of similar challenges in the UK. There was world overcapacity in their market and expanding sales through supermarkets, with the threat of more price competition should the product be used as a loss leader. The retail structure encouraged the dominance of own-label, with brands accounting for less than 14% of the market. More widely there was the prospect of decline within the market because of the rise in casual attire, epitomized by jeans, and the tendency for women's legs to be covered by clothes.

Pretty Polly met these challenges with a five-year plan. They needed to raise volume by 25% and increase the proportion of their branded sales from 17% to 80%. They wanted to get into the rapidly expanding grocery sector but didn't want to alienate the drapery stores, which still accounted for 26% of their sales. In response to this they set up a sub-brand – Galaxy Pretty Polly – for the grocery trade. This had a more limited selection than was available in drapery outlets and so helped maintain the confidence of this sector, rather than alienate it through a simple expansion of the products they were selling into the grocery end of the business. Coupled with this was a distribution strategy involving a gradual withdrawal from the static and declining areas of the market: conventional chain stores and wholesale outlets.

These strategic moves were all designed to cope with the evolution of the distribution structure of the market. However, there were always the changing perceptions of the consumer to be taken into account, swayed as they were by the fickle winds of fashion. This challenge Pretty Polly met head-on with the proposition "Pretty Polly brings back lovely legs", a clear attack on jeans, which, of course, did not allow legs to shine. All this combined to raise profits in four years from £0.281 million to £4.036 million. The detailed distribution plans paid off too, as the drapery share actually increased in this period from 25% to 34%, while in the grocery sector it rose from 9% to 20.6%. And it was their branded product which was leading this success, with the proportion of sales with the Pretty Polly logo rising from 17% to 60%.

THE PRODUCT MIGHT BE RIGHT, BUT YOU HAVE TO KNOW HOW IT'S RIGHT

With Dr Beckmann Rescue Oven Cleaner in the UK a radical revamp was required as, after eighteen months on the market, it was making no impression, particularly in the face of Mr Muscle, which was synonymous with oven cleaning. Although this latter brand was highly effective, it was unpleasant to use – the resulting fumes sometimes choking the user and getting into their lungs. The actual cleaning process could take ages and there was the possibility of getting burned. Also Mr Muscle was available only in aerosol form and was perceived to be environmentally dangerous. The bottom line, however, was a market share of 64.67% for Mr Muscle compared with 19.24% for Dr Beckmann. In addition, Dr Beckmann had the added constraint of being a third more expensive than Mr Muscle.

Research pointed out that modern women were more than ever concerned about their appearance. They were not prepared to put up with products that were harmful to their skin, which contained toxins or didn't fit their self-image. Most household products had evolved to take these issues into account, but oven cleaners hadn't. Dr Beckmann could be presented as a more natural choice as it had a unique gel formulation that clung to the surface and used enzymes to naturally break down the encrusted, burnt-on food rather than corroding it away with highly caustic chemicals.

"Modern women wanted to cut corners but do it with their conscience intact"

Modern women wanted to cut corners but do it with their conscience intact. Dr Beckmann was the cleaner for them. It was effective, safe, pleasant, low-stress and fast. These positives were refined into the unique position of cleaning ovens and being kind to hands, a strategy that cut through the market with an increase of 68% in the value of the brand over a year. Brand share rose from 23% to 31% in fifteen months while Mr Muscle's fell by 13.4%.

WHEN TIME TRANSFORMS

Dr Beckmann's success was due to unearthing inherent product advantages that had always been there, but had not been exploited. Sometimes a small improvement in a product can result in a quantum shift in its position – as in the case of the Eurostar train from London to Paris and Brussels, when its journey time was reduced by twenty minutes. This doesn't seem that much, and nor did it to the users of Eurostar – except some business travellers. To the leisure market it meant nothing.

To project it as something meaningful, this shorter journey time needed to trigger a fundamental reappraisal of Eurostar. Rather than positioning it as different from airlines, the strategy had to assert its superiority – which led to the concept of "Fly Eurostar". And fly it did, with a net increase in revenue of £13.6 million.

This showed how length of time can be the base for a strong assault. In the case of Purolator Courier in Canada it was an actual time in the day. They were having a hard time in the midst of a recession with increased competition. The top companies were seen as similar in satisfying the core needs of consumers and so any differentiation was difficult. Purolator's research had identified the 9 a.m. Day Starter service as their product with the most potential. It demonstrated that Purolator put the consumer first by responding to and anticipating their needs. The basis for this position came from psychology and the concept of the circadian rhythms of the body. This focuses on the patterns the body goes through each day and studies that have shown that a person's productivity decreases as the day advances. Also, from a purely intuitive viewpoint, it was hypothesized that, with the advance of the day, a person's stress levels would rise and their feelings of control would slip away. Consumers agreed with this.

Consequently, for the senders, the 9 a.m. arrival meant that their package would get undivided attention and for the receivers there was a window to focus on it before things got out of control, or, as Purolator put it, "before the day got to them". They were then able to build on the commitment and leadership that Day Start demonstrated to potential customers. Sales of Day Start increased by 27% within a year and helped raise the overall business of Purolator by 10%.

SIMPLE MATHS MAKES SIMPLE GROWTH

With this simple approach Purolator was able to advance, but the elements that went into this position were quite complex. In the case of Motrin analgesic in Canada the key to its success was the difference between two and three – not exactly rocket science, but profoundly effective nevertheless. Motrin is an ibuprofen and wasn't making any

---

"In the case of Motrin analgesic in Canada the key to its success was the difference between two and three"

---

progress against Advil, the market leader, as there was no product differentiation nor innovation available. Pain relief would seem a simple area, but given that it is such a personal problem, each individual sees their pain as unique and wants to choose pain relief based on their own personal assessment of the degree of their pain.

This basic idiosyncrasy was Advil's Achilles heel. They offered only two levels of pain relief: Regular 200mg and Extra 400mg. Motrin offered three: Regular 200mg, Extra

300mg and Super Strength 400mg. So, with a simple numerical advantage of three versus two, Motrin was able to offer the promise of "whatever the level of pain, Motrin has your relief". And the market numbers responded to this simple maths, with Motrin's share rising by 40% in just one year.

In Motrin's case giving three as opposed to two proved to be crucial, but in some cases, while giving can appear generous, the receiving can be even greater, as in the case of BT in the UK. Their position in the market did not seem to lend itself to giving; from holding a monopoly of telephone calls they had lost 10% share in the first ten years since this position was lost and a further 20% in the succeeding five years – the pace of erosion was quickening.

One response to this was BT becoming the first to lock customers in by offering unlimited calls for a flat monthly fee. In addition they gave a free answering service, called 1571 after the number that was dialled to access it. The question, as with anything given away free, was how would this help the bottom line. The answer came from an understanding of the product, as income was generated by the calls taken and, more significantly, by the returned calls, which would not otherwise have occurred. The result was that over 9.5 million households joined the BT Together packages and over 5 million became 1571 customers. Also the rate of decline was slowed substantially from 9.2% p.a. to 4.5%.

THE GAP BETWEEN TWO CHAIRS IS NOT ALWAYS FOR FALLING INTO

Sometimes brands occupy a position where they feel they are being pincered by two larger competitors and their ultimate fate appears that of being squeezed to death. Just as something can be caught between two presses, however, so it can pop up, as happened to Vogue Furniture of Scotland. They found a bit of "wiggle room". Vogue was a small independent furniture retailer with only three stores and an annual turnover of £19 million. For long they had to compete against the higher-end quality of the John Lewis department stores. Then they were hemmed in on their other flank by the arrival of the more price-competitive DFS and Ikea, both of which had clearly established brand positions.

Vogue's loyal customer base was ageing. Older customers tended to replace furniture less often and Vogue was underperforming against the age group with the most potential – the 25 to 34-year-olds – which was itself declining because of demographic changes. This was all compounded by recession, in which new furniture sales was one of the first areas to be hit. Sales had shrunk by 7% from their peak three years previously.

In research it was found that all consumers wanted to buy the best of both worlds: furniture that looked good and didn't fall apart instantly. The balance between these two factors would vary. John Lewis and other more established

brands were thought to offer robust but less stylish
furniture. Ikea was viewed as modern and stylish but more
disposable. Consequently the ideal positioning would
combine the build quality of John Lewis with the design

"**Style** with substance"

---

style of Ikea – a niche for Vogue to slip into using the
proposition of "style with substance". And substance was
the result in terms of sales. The company had its most
successful winter sales period in their history with a rise of
30% in sales.

OVERALL

Awareness of the product and what it can offer the
consumer is essential. Sometimes this means unearthing
winning characteristics of the product which no one had
previously had the wit to recognize – as in the case of Dr
Beckmann's oven cleaner or the simple mathematical fact
that three is better than two, exploited so ingeniously by
Motrin.

One of the most challenging aspects of making a product
into a successful brand is the ability to spot what appears to
be an inconsequential detail and appreciate the significance
it can have in making the brand truly different for the
consumer – such as the way in which Eurostar transformed

twenty minutes into a totally different point of comparison or in which Purolator built so much on just one delivery time.

What is also important is an ability to take in the many dynamics that revolve around a product and the ability to see it in a context that is different from the stereotypical role it is expected to play or be consigned to – as in the case of Swan Vesta matches. In addition there needs to be the appreciation that quite simple changes can make a big difference to consumer perceptions, as happened with Crown paint and Source yogurt, as well as more fundamental reappraisals and improvements, such as those wrought by Giggles nappies.

It is not just the physical characteristics of the product which can be transformed into making a difference, however, but also its emotional footprint. This was recognized by Alexander Keith in Canada and the successful focusing by Polo on what were seen as inherent Volkswagen strengths.

Finally, in the development of a brand as much as in any other endeavour, there needs to be sufficient flexibility to recognize the gift sometimes bestowed by serendipity and to use it in the way that Weet-bix did to such effect in Australia.

2

IT'S THE CONSUMER, STUPID

It might seem a good idea at the time, but it has to connect with the consumer

"Often that link is actually a cord within the consumer that can be pulled – but it has to be found"

However good a product might seem on paper and even in research, it still has to make a connection with the consumer to be successful. Often that link is actually a cord within the consumer that can be pulled – but it has to be found. The consumer needs to be understood in terms of their needs and, sometimes more importantly, their quirks and foibles. A good illustration of this was the casual observation of his neighbours' dogs by Mr Hosaka, the Principal Project Director at Nissan. He noticed that people tended to avoid petting his neighbour's tosa dogs, a Japanese breed developed as a fighting dog. They loved, however, to make a fuss over his terrier. This led Mr Hosaka to design the highly successful Nissan Micra as a car that was lively and friendly rather than sharp and aggressive.

SOMETIMES IT'S THE PRODUCER WHO LIMITS THE BRAND, NOT THE CONSUMER

Such a connection can sometimes be made by what looks like a mere sleight of hand or semantic trick. Pine-Sol in Canada is a household cleaner which was present in homes, but was losing out because it was used only occasionally for heavy-duty jobs. They discovered that women would identify different levels of "clean", from when a friend just popped in to when their mother-in-law came for a family event.

Consistent with these findings, a new level of clean was created for Pine-Sol which was in tune with its strengths, but shed the heavy-duty connotations. This was articulated as "thorough clean". This seemingly simple shift resulted in volume growing at 5% ahead of the market while competition declined and Pine-Sol didn't lose out to increased competitive activity in the market, whereas Mr Clean, its main competitor, did.

Overcoming such stereotypes regarding the role of products can appear insurmountable when the beliefs of a mother with regard to the treatment of her children are concerned. Lipton chicken noodle soup in Canada had encouraging news from research indicating that children loved their soup. Any rejoicing was dampened, however, by the reaction of mothers who certainly knew their kids liked it, but didn't want to serve it too often as they thought overfamiliarity might make their children tire of it.

Such a view was entirely reasonable – for an adult. Children, in contrast, will never tire of something they like. This truth was well illustrated in the children's TV show *Blues Clues*, which broadcast the same programme every day of the week without any decline in the enthusiasm of its young viewers. Lipton reminded mothers that when children like something,

---

"Children, in contrast, will never tire of something they like"

---

they like it a lot – a feeling undimmed by repetition. Within one year a 2% decline in volume had been turned into a rise of 9%, the first growth of the brand in fourteen years. The resistance of the purchaser, in the person of the mother, had been overcome by the idiosyncratic attitudes of the consumer, the child.

WHERE THE CONSUMER LEADS, THE BRAND SHOULD FOLLOW

The opposite of overcoming barriers is actually letting the consumer guide the brand into solutions discovered by the brand keeping its antennae finely tuned and interpreting the signal from the consumer with the skill of a code-breaker. Ross Oriental Express is a frozen food which was relaunched on an "authentic" platform that did not work as it was not credible for the brand. When consumers talked about Oriental Express, however, they used language reserved for real food, describing taste, textures and appetite appeal even though it was a convenience frozen food. Combined with this information was a finding that the amount of effort involved in cooking seemed to improve food values – the more effort put in, the more "real" was the resulting food.

"**The more effort put in,** the more 'real' was the resulting food"

The splicing of these two strands came with the use of the stir-fry method. This was an involving way of cooking, appealing to all the senses, with the sizzling of the frying, the colours of the vegetables and the smell. These elements helped position Oriental Express under the umbrella of real food and divorce it from its true nature as a convenience frozen food. They were articulated as "fast involving oriental food". As an added refinement, Oriental Express needed to reflect the basic need the consumer had when buying frozen – speed and satiation with an extra edge of excitement. This resulted in the phrase "a quick feast for all your senses".

HEALTHY BODY, HEALTHY SALES

This scratching around for a positioning was also, rather fittingly, the root of a revival in the fortunes of the Canadian egg market. In the 1960s the annual consumption per capita had been around 22 dozen, yet by 1995 this figure had fallen to 14.27 dozen. One of the key ingredients in this decline was the perception that eating eggs could lead to cholesterol problems, a negative compounded by the fitness craze and health consciousness. These beliefs were largely without substance. Eggs did not contribute to increased blood cholesterol for 80% of Canadians. The key element of marketing, however, is that, as it revolves around the consumer's outlook, it deals solely in perceptions, not reality.

"The key element of marketing is that, as it revolves around the consumer's outlook, it deals solely in perceptions, not reality"

Efforts had been put behind extolling the versatility of eggs, but research showed this was preaching to the converted and that health continued to be the major barrier. There was the dilemma, however, that openly confronting the cholesterol issue could perpetuate misconceptions – with accusations of "thou doth protest too much". The most constructive approach appeared to be not to attempt to dispel the health concerns, but rather to defuse them.

When egg buyers were interviewed they reported a large variety of associations with eggs such as convenience and versatility. None said, however, that they regarded them as natural. Yet when asked specifically whether they saw them as natural they all responded in the affirmative – it was something that was so taken for granted it wasn't worth mentioning. This fed into the strategic concept of "nature doesn't make food that's bad for you", and so the notion that eggs are nature's food became a proxy for "good for you".

The result of this was that average consumption of eggs increased by six eggs per person in the first year, the first reversal of decline in seventeen years. There was a further increase of two eggs in the following year. This was in a climate where other foods tainted by concerns over fat and cholesterol – such as red meat and milk – continued their decline.

TAKE EACH STEP AT A TIME

Looking at health from the other direction was the driving force behind Nicorette, who approached their strategy not from the viewpoint of the opportunities that consumer perceptions could offer, but rather from the limitations that needed to be recognized. Many brands in their market claimed to provide smokers with the benefit of being able to completely give up smoking. This was seen by many smokers as an excessive promise which could not be fulfilled and so put them off. Nicorette chose attainable objectives, an approach enshrined in the attitude of football clubs taking each game at a time or golfers each hole at a time. Nicorette chose to take each cigarette at a time. This could be seen as a more honest and attainable goal, winning each individual battle with cigarettes rather than promising outright victory in the war.

It also chimed with smokers' feelings, as most could not imagine being able to stop smoking cigarettes altogether, but could think of giving up one or two a day. Rather than having a mountain to climb, they would have only a series of hills to stroll over, and so felt more empowered in their efforts. Empowerment was the result for Nicorette's sales. They increased from $194 million to $295 million in four years, expanding from seven to sixteen advertised countries and becoming clear market leader.

TO GET CONSUMERS, PICK THE RIGHT ONES

The cases above involve health as a spur for the brand; in the case of health clubs it can be a spur for the consumer. At the time, six of the ten top-selling videos in the UK were for home exercise, and 86% of the population were not using health clubs. This group was the target the Edinburgh Health Club went after.

The profile of health club users suggested that the highest potential lay among young upmarket men. They were already using health clubs, however, and the Edinburgh Health Club saw the greatest potential in non-users, more specifically an older female target market – the sort of people who were "going for the burn" with the Jane Fonda exercise videos popular at the time. In addition there were the guilty couch potatoes who had once been trim and fit, but for whom circumstances had conspired to remove exercise from their lives. There were also senior citizens who were seen as good for off-peak. The greatest barrier to entry for this target appeared to be the fear factor of being looked down on by the beautiful people they imagined used health clubs.

"I can do something about my fitness or fatness without looking like a prat"

The Edinburgh Health Club put out the message that it was the place where "I can do something about my fitness or fatness without looking like a prat." Within two years new members had risen by 330% and, from a small base, off-peak had increased by 1,130%. This was all achieved while maintaining a premium of 23% over the general health club market (£480 versus an average of £390) at a time of recession, resulting in a rise in profits of 174%.

By going after a different set of consumers, Edinburgh Health Club managed to expand its business, and this can work on much more prosaic levels, as with Irving Home Furnaces in Canada. On the Atlantic side of Canada, 40% of homes had furnaces that were over ten years old and 25% had furnaces over fifteen years old. This resulted in considerable inefficiencies for the consumer, as the earlier models wasted as much as 40 cents in the dollar on heating oil. By contrast, the monthly savings after installing a new high-efficiency furnace more than outweighed Irving's monthly furnace lease cost, so that a new furnace would pay for itself.

Despite this compelling rationale the furnaces were still not an item that people chose to buy, but rather something they bought out of necessity and tended to regard as a grudge purchase. Consumer apathy was fuelled by fears of high upfront replacement costs. There was, however, one facet of the market which helped Irving direct its efforts – there was a direct correlation between the age of the furnace and the age of the homeowner. This led to Irving targeting homeowners over 50, which produced growth in sales of 50% in one three-month autumn period.

LIGHTENING THE BURDEN OF DOMESTIC MAN

On another household front a simple change in the target tapped a well that competition had ignored. In Canada, paint brands had traditionally targeted women and based their arguments on the aesthetic appeal of decoration. This was on the reasonable premise that women decided on the projects and colours used. This consideration left out, however, a crucial part in the process – its execution. Men bought the materials and did the painting, presumably under the careful supervision of their wives.

Many of these men might be proud of the results, but hated the actual painting process, which was often done under duress. Consequently Crown Diamond targeted men with the promise that "Crown Diamond takes the pain out of painting". This position provided some balm for their bottom line with average sales per retailer rising by 23% in two years. At the same time they managed to maintain the ratio in favour of their premium sub-brands, despite branded paint being under heavy pressure from own-label paints.

Such careful targeting can often be a route to success, but often it's the purchaser rather than the end consumer of the product who's important. This is clearly the case with brands for animals, as their purchasing power is somewhat limited and it is their owners who shell out. Frontline Plus in the USA stops fleas and ticks from climbing aboard pets. It had been successfully launched with a campaign that focused on a pet-loving vet. It was, however, facing a threat in the form of a new product from its main competitor, and it also wanted to reach new purchasers for whom the flea/tick issue was not a top priority.

In concept testing a strong proposition was that Frontline Plus didn't just protect pets, it protected homes and families too. This focused on fleas as not just a problem for the pets, but rather as an environmental nuisance. It was presenting the purchaser with a problem they didn't know they had. And it worked. Share was maintained and slightly increased in the face of the competition's new product, which largely cannibalized its other brand, and Frontline Plus's sales reached an all-time high.

DRILLING DOWN INTO HEALTH

One of the most defined and particular areas in health is teeth, and Colgate has long been dominant in the toothpaste market in many countries. In the UK, however, they faced a significant challenge from Sainsbury, a large supermarket chain, which was going to launch an own-label dental-care range. They had already had considerable success with their Classic Cola and also with own-label detergents. Consumers would probably give the new Sainsbury product a try as their core beliefs were that most toothpastes were much the same and that better dental protection was due to things other than toothpaste.

Closer examination of the context showed that even committed Sainsbury shoppers were more likely to buy some manufactured brands in preference to own-label – these were in specific categories, such as medical products. There was a feeling of a greater risk involved in buying the retailer's own brand in these fields as it might deliver lower product quality owing to a lack of sufficient expertise in the field.

To capitalize on this perception, Colgate sought to position itself more as a brand with "medical" benefits and increase its perceived dental expertise beyond the reach of competitors. They used the statement "Colgate is the better protector" and were able to support this with the fact that they had been making toothpaste for 120 years. Also Colgate didn't make it for anyone else (i.e. own-label) and more dentists chose it for their families than any other toothpaste (hardly surprising as it had been clear market leader for several decades).

Such a position successfully blunted the edge of Sainsbury's new toothpaste range to the extent that Colgate transformed defence into attack. Colgate's value share rose after Sainsbury's launch from 28.5% to 32.9%, sales increased by 20% and volume rose 13%, while margins advanced by 7%.

RECOGNIZING THE CONSUMER'S CONTEXT

In looking at the market in which a brand operates it's not just understanding the particular context of that market which is important, but also understanding the broader context of the consumer. LaSalle Bank of Chicago wanted to target those with investable assets of more than $500,000, around two million households. Although they were the second-biggest bank in Chicago, they didn't have the same reputation for managing individuals' wealth as their competitors. Their forte was serving medium-sized businesses, and they were the most highly regarded business bank in Chicago.

Their target was defined as "the working wealthy" – those who tend not to act rich as they started life with modest means. In general they didn't categorize themselves in terms of money, but rather in terms of their lives as successful business managers. They had high expectations of their business partners, which would transfer to their personal lives. Often they would rely on the same trusted advisers and partners – lawyers and accountants – for their personal needs as they used in business.

LaSalle Bank realized they were in a position that could include them in this axis. They articulated it by putting forward the proposition that personal finances would benefit from working with a bank that understood the needs of people managing successful businesses. This resulted in private banking deposits rising by 24% – against an objective of 15% – and assets managed by LaSalle wealth management rising nearly 10%.

"The key to resolving this dilemma was to bring focus into their efforts"

Success for LaSalle resulted from pulling on a particular consumer cord. With the Bank of America's mortgage campaign in the USA it came from recognizing a previously unappreciated requirement. As a full-service consumer bank they couldn't offer the lowest rates and were outspent by their mortgage company competitors. The key to resolving this dilemma was to bring focus into their efforts. They concentrated on the repeat homebuyer. These customers were more likely to be approved for a mortgage; they were also one of the least-targeted groups by Bank of America's competitors. They had already experienced the mortgage process and knew what a hassle it could be and the amount of paperwork involved. Bank of America promised 80% less paperwork.

In gauging the success of this strategy the Mortgage Brokers Association of America has an index that is used as a benchmark for mortgage applications, much as the Dow Jones is used for the stock market. Bank of America had consistently underperformed this index by as much as 14% before the change of strategy, and after its adoption the bank consistently exceeded the index, by as much as 59%.

FASHION IS FROTH SO THE BRAND NEEDS TO RIDE THE SURF

Even the mightiest of market oaks can have their roots nibbled by the flighty fancies of fashion. Marks and Spencer (M&S) in the UK had such an experience in the lingerie market. Its share was five times that of its nearest competitor and 40% of all women in the UK shopped for lingerie in M&S each year. Yet the average number of transactions per month had declined by 2.65%.

M&S was not capitalizing on the fashion-led growth in the sector. Although it had the product, consumers viewed what it had to offer as functional. It was a destination for "mission" shoppers who would go there for specific items, rather than for browsers, who would come in on the off-chance of being surprised or lured into getting something frivolous. At the other end of the spectrum M&S was losing out to discounters who had grown by a third in two years.

To combat these factors they needed to establish a position that capitalized on their key strengths of quality and range. In addition M&S needed to appeal to the 35–45 age group without alienating their core 45+ customers. To help inform their decisions M&S conducted some research. This revealed interesting shifts in the attitude of women to lingerie. They were treating their lingerie in the same way as their clothes, looking for a comparable range of variations. What they wore underneath their clothes changed the way they felt, in much the same way as the clothes they wore to be seen in – others didn't see them, but the wearer felt the effect. It was a private and personal form of self-expression. The language of lingerie was something hidden, but, maybe partly because of this, it was the ultimate expression of femininity.

"A place where a woman could find not just 'something for you', but 'something for every you'"

M&S was able to respond to these attitudes with the widest range of lingerie of any retailer, and they could feed and inspire this multidimensional inner self of women in a way barred to others. This was the reality, but not the consumer perception. M&S had to articulate this strength in a way that would establish it clearly in the minds of consumers. They did this by describing M&S as "lingerie heaven", literally articulating the findings of the research by describing it as a place where a woman could find not just "something for you", but "something for every you". This was encapsulated in the proposition "In Marks & Spencer Lingerie Heaven you'll find underwear for every you."

The consequence of this was marketing heaven for M&S. The lines advertised with this message showed an average 44% increase on the base week and an overall increase of £6.6 million over the course of the campaign. M&S lingerie overall grew by 4% in a market that was shrinking by 1% and there was an increase of 1.3% in overall market share.

IDENTIFYING CONSUMER IDENTITY

With many consumers there is the phenomenon of exterior validation whereby they feel that what they are wearing/using helps give them some identity in relation to others, something most pronounced with fashion and luxury goods. A less self-regarding trait, however, is the desire to identify with a group, something well known in the school playground with peer groups and in the support of sports teams. In the case of the Canadian Football League (CFL) it was a lifeline.

Sports marketing in Canada had made substantial gains in credibility and profitability. The CFL failed to climb aboard this trend, however, and each year the media declared that year to be their last. Their demographics pointed to a gradual demise as more than half their viewers were over 50. CFL's previous positioning had been "radically Canadian", which had been differentiating, but not in a helpful way. It focused on the differences between American and Canadian football in a context in which 70% of CFL fans were also NFL fans. In doing this it engaged in the pointless exercise of forcing people to choose one league over another. On stepping back from this, it was realized that the true competition was not other forms of football, but other forms of entertainment, particularly other professional sports.

In general, the fans' interest in professional sports was based on winning. This in turn was often locally based – if your team was not playing your emotional investment was not so high and so the outcome was less interesting. The characteristics of the CFL responded to these feelings as they had only eight teams, so they often played each other, which made for intense rivalries. To capitalize on this the CFL came up with the line: "It's not just football, it's personal". This helped galvanize interest, and in the first year sponsorship revenue increased by 18% and brought in sponsors from new categories. Also, interest among younger males increased substantially, with TV viewing figures for the 18–34 age group rising by 32% and for men over eighteen rising by 25%.

Identity operates at much more profound emotional levels than relationships with football teams, in particular when it relates to one's past emotional identity. This was exploited by Diet Pepsi in Canada. Their share had stagnated since the launch of a reformulated product, and if the brand couldn't improve its position, then Pepsi was faced with the expensive prospect of launching Pepsi One, which had already been introduced in the USA.

The problem was that, as they got older, regular Pepsi drinkers were switching to Diet Coke, not transferring to Diet Pepsi. Diet Pepsi was hampered by having the same image as regular Pepsi, an image crafted to appeal to young, open-minded Pepsi drinkers, less relevant to the key 25 to 34-year-old target for diet colas. Coke, with a more conservative image, was better able to facilitate a smooth transition to its diet brand. Diet Pepsi was further hampered by not being able to fight against its parent brand's image; rather it was having to make regular Pepsi imagery work for it.

The identity of the target market itself was key to the resolution of this dilemma. They recognized and accepted that they were "maturing", but regretted the loss of the crazy and irresponsible days of their youth, which, after all, weren't so far away. This yearning provided a bridge for Diet Pepsi to connect them to the youthful heritage of Pepsi. They understood that they might be maturing in age and responsibility, but felt that they would always remain young at heart. The encapsulation of this promise was the phrase "young at heart".

Not only was this a bridge between the two brands, but it proved to be a bridge to growth for Diet Pepsi. Their share rose from 4.8% to 5.1%, all at the expense of Diet Coke.

They continued to grow to 5.6% versus 5.7% for Diet Coke. In addition this success made a big saving in costs and risk as it removed the need to launch Pepsi One in Canada. In fact the success achieved by Diet Pepsi was transferred back to the USA, where support for Diet Pepsi was regalvanized.

CHANGED CONSUMER ATTITUDES, CHANGED OPPORTUNITIES

As demonstrated by the case of M&S lingerie, the changing approach of consumers can leave a brand behind if it is not spotted. By the same token, awareness can give the brand a head start and act as the foundation for enduring success. Kellogg's Coco Pops were diminishing in importance. They were not supported by marketing and were losing their appeal to children. It was at this point that general research across the Kellogg's brands suggested there was a change in parental attitudes, with a greater readiness to indulge children by paying a bit extra for food and snacks that they regarded as treats. This meant that parents were more willing to provide the cereals their children asked for.

These trends gave an underlying reason to support Coco Pops and the possibility of it forging a separate identity from Rice Krispies, the simple puffed rice cereal. Also, the word "Pops" helped communicate the explosive fun qualities of the brand. The actual strategy that these elements led to was to tell children (and their mothers) that Coco Pops were delicious and fun. Within six months of this position being adopted in two test areas, sales increased by 72% and 95%.

TURNING OFF CAN TURN ON

Most successful marketing connects with the consumer. The assumption is that such a connection should be in a positive vein. A negative link can also be turned to advantage, however. This was evident in the strategy adopted by the police recruitment campaign in the UK, which, rather than trying to encourage and persuade, aimed at actively discouraging and dissuading.

"**The police recruitment campaign in** the UK, rather than trying to encourage and persuade, aimed at actively discouraging and dissuading"

Such an approach sounds perverse; there was, however, an ingenious logic underlying it. When looking for new police officers, only one person in 4,000 needed to be recruited, so a highly specific minority needed to be targeted. The filtering process in recruiting can be wasteful and inefficient, so anything that could dissuade those who were unlikely to be appropriate candidates saved expense. In addition, there was a low public opinion of the police, resulting in low morale within the force.

Rather than overtly singing the praises of the police, the position adopted was one of well-known people admitting they didn't have the qualities needed to be a police officer. The strategy was to have messages that acted as a counterpoint to each person's strengths, with world boxing champion Lennox Lewis admitting he would struggle to restrain himself from punching a wife-beater, and Bob Geldof unable to separate a child from its abusive parents. These were all summarized by the line: "I couldn't. Could you?" The very admission of defeat incited consideration. Research was conducted removing the "I couldn't" part of the equation and the response was much reduced.

The result was the most efficient recruitment campaign in the history of the Effectiveness Awards, with the valuable extra dimensions of an improvement in public perception of the police and in their self-image. The campaign cost £15 million, but was reckoned to have saved the UK taxpayer at least £30 million through the increased efficiency of the recruitment process.

THE DREAM IS OF THE CUSTOMER STAYING; SOMETIMES THEY DREAM THE SAME

The unusual aspect of the police recruitment campaign was that it sought to dissuade rather than persuade many of those who came into contact with the proposition. This was also the case with Frizzell Insurance in the UK, and they had the added bonus of being able to arrive at a position mirroring their objectives and appealing directly to consumers.

They were under threat from Direct Line insurance, but, as a defence, they had a lot of loyal customers – nine out of ten renewed their policy annually with Frizzell. There had, however, been a slowdown in enquiries. In addressing this situation Frizzell felt they had to appeal to the "right" people and discourage everyone else. This was because these other consumers would be difficult to satisfy on price, as Frizzell products were priced around 5% above the competition. Also, Frizzell did not want to attract too many customers who would be more likely to claim. They wanted to position themselves away from other insurers.

Their customers were conservative, loyal, risk averse and cautious. For them, loyalty was equal to good service and a good-value product. These were irrelevant to a high-risk consumer, who was more interested in financial deals. Consequently the consumer position Frizzell arrived at mirrored the company's own desires – "when you join Frizzell you will never want to leave". The response of consumers to this helped consolidate the brand to the tune of £188 million, which was the price that was paid for the company by Liverpool Victoria only four years after it had been sold for £108 million.

OVERALL

Sometimes the idiosyncrasies of people can be infuriating and sometimes they can be endearing. In terms of developing a strategy for a brand they are precious because they tap into the emotional heartland, which is the soil in which a brand can most successfully grow.

As in the case of lingerie with M&S, these are sometimes quite fluid concepts which then set into concrete foundations for brand growth and strength. It is also important that those developing the strategy put themselves in the minds of their consumers, so they can recognize opportunities such as that provided for Lipton chicken noodle soup by children's failure to get bored with something they like, or the fundamental view of eggs as being healthy.

In many respects the brand is simply tailored to the dimensions of the consumers' perceptions for, if not the *raison d'être* of a brand, they are at least the reason for its success.

3

EMOTIONAL ROLLER-COASTER

What sets a brand apart from the functional attributes of a product is the consumer choosing it on emotional rather than just rational grounds

Emotion is usually the springboard for a product to leap beyond its functional status and arrive at the more fabled existence of a brand. The interesting point about emotion is that it is not something that can manifest itself in a physical way, but rather it has to derive from a seed that has grown or been cultivated in the mind of the individual. Often it is the intangible added value which transforms a product into a brand, much as, in fairy tales, a kiss turns a frog into a prince. In marketing, the kiss can be provided by the transforming effect of an insight into the emotions a brand can call on or create.

"**The intangible added value which** transforms a product into a brand, much as, in fairy tales, a kiss turns a frog into a prince"

CARING CAN COUNT

Sometimes the move to emotion is simple, as in the case of Nissan Canada. They discovered through research that buying a car was a decision based on more than product merits. The differences between competitive models had become more subtle. They summed this up by saying that consumers were looking for a relationship with a car company.

"Individual success was dependent on shared goals and connectedness with others"

Their response was to set up a department of 30 people dedicated to customer satisfaction combined with a warranty/support programme, all summarized as "the Satisfaction Commitment". This was to present Nissan as a car company with a commitment to the consumer which went beyond building state-of-the-art cars. Such an undertaking touched a chord as Nissan's market share rose from 3.4% to 3.8% and their volume grew by 1% in a market where overall volume went down by 10%.

IT'S GOOD TO SHARE

So goes the saying told to us as children, and which parents continue to preach. Yet sharing is an activity which has become a catalyst for brands in the most unlikely cases. Banking is a field where the exercise of reason is perceived as supreme, yet First Citizens Bank in the USA showed how emotion could provide essential leverage. They were experiencing competition from bigger banks in their area. Their focus was on families that had children and their own home.

The way banks spoke to people was often in terms of their individual dreams. The dreams of the target First Citizens had chosen, however, were rarely particular to them. They were shared with their spouses, children, siblings, friends and co-workers. Individual success was dependent on shared goals and connectedness with others. This insight led First Citizens to show how financial products can have a ripple effect. As financial products can intimidate people, First Citizens wanted to show how the opposite can be true, and how they could have an immediate and intimate impact.

Such considerations resulted in putting forward the bank as one that would help consumers by "doing something amazing". A deceptively simple distillation of their insights, yet one that increased First Citizens' new chequing accounts, the core of new banking relationships, by 7.5%.

The importance of shared emotions tapped into by First Citizen was also brought into play by Bud Light in Canada. It had been launched in Ontario, but had not been supported and had drifted into obscurity, with a market share of less than 0.5%. Most beers were targeting entry-level drinkers, young men aged 19–24. They were undoubtedly the heaviest drinkers per capita, but, in the light beer sector, 75% of the volume came from drinkers aged over 25. The younger age group was in fact more likely to reject light beers.

Despite its prominence, no beer was focusing on this 25-plus group. The route to addressing them was provided by a minor emotional dichotomy that existed within this group. Being guys, they had an inherent desire to get out with their buddies and drink beer. The older men, however, felt that they had to balance this urge with their responsibilities. Consequently they couldn't go out whenever they wanted to, which made the times when they could more valuable. Bud Light played on this through the proposition that it would do anything to get you out with your buddies. In two years its market share nearly doubled and it became one of the fastest-growing brands in Ontario.

Moving from drink to food, the leverage offered by shared feelings was also evident in the revival of Pizza Hut in the UK. They had answered market pressures with short-term promotional activity. This was initially successful, but wore out over time as the promotions were easily replicable by the competition and many small operators reacted aggressively. All this led to more discounting and a downward revenue spiral.

"It can't be that great if they're going to give you an extra one free"

The price-cutting had undermined Pizza Hut's quality credentials. The brand had become associated with food that was eaten only when you couldn't get or couldn't be bothered to buy something else. This was embodied in comments such as "I wouldn't cross the road unless there was an offer" and "It can't be that great if they're going to give you an extra one free".

Consequently it was important to build value back into the brand. The main target was lapsed users; two-thirds of the UK population had used Pizza Hut. They had to re-establish some relevance for Pizza Hut by creating a clear pizza occasion. The way pizza was viewed by consumers was as a shared food which induced a relaxed familiarity, bringing people together. Pizza Hut set out to project an image of relaxed fun meals among friends or close family. The result of this positioning was an increase in revenue per store of over 21%.

SHOW, DON'T TELL

This approach by Pizza Hut tapped into an emotional vein that already existed in relation to a product. Sometimes there is nothing intrinsically emotional about a product, but this can be exploited either by adopting a position or by answering the consumers' desire for one. This latter element was the dynamic in the case of the Toyota Matrix in Canada. Toyota had success in the market with an approach based on the rational promises of price, quality, value for money, reliability and reputation. This "telling" approach did not, however, sit well with the target for the Matrix, whose attitude was "show me, don't tell me".

The result was that Toyota positioned the Matrix as the rebel of the Toyota family and created an unconventional personality for it. They positioned the Matrix as being unlike any other Toyota, focusing on key motivators of exterior styling, performance, roadholding and handling to make it appear cool and desirable. Its share reached 23.4% as against 16.6% for the Pontiac Vibe, which was the same basic car with minor aesthetic variations. Within sixteen months the Matrix was outselling the Vibe by over 50%.

THE PHILOSOPHER'S STONE: SOMETIMES THE BRAND CAN TURN BASE METAL INTO GOLD

Imposing emotions in the way the Matrix did can be a strong catalyst for a brand, but digging them up can sometimes reveal even deeper roots. Bassett's Liquorice Allsorts are a UK variety of liquorice-based sweets coming in different shapes and colours. Their sales reached a peak in 1956, but, 30 years later, had fallen to less than half their previous volume. They had a shrinking consumer base which was increasingly old and downmarket. The product itself was perceived as bland, unexciting and undifferentiated, with little to justify the price premium over other liquorice sweets.

Research found that Bassett's had a well-defined emotional role as the choice people made when feeling childish. Many felt that being sensible and adult could be tedious and that scoffing Bassett's was an amusing way of regressing to a childish state. The taste, texture and colours of the sweets were unique and they had unusual play value for adults –

"Being sensible and adult could be tedious"

they were almost like an adult toy. In addition they had a moreish quality, as it was difficult for most users to eat one without going on to finish the whole bag. This manic approach was often a source of amusement.

All of these elements were melded into a position facilitated by the one property Bassett's had – Bertie Bassett, a figure made up from the sweets. This anthropomorphic character and the moreish nature of the sweets led to the line: "eat any more and you'll turn into one". This led to an increase in the share of Bassett's from 56.3% to 62% in a market that grew by 19%, while the brand still managed to maintain its price premium.

In the case of Bassett's the success came from digging up the emotional roots of the brand, whereas sometimes the emotional cues can be found by just looking at the roots of the product, as with Murphy's stout in the UK, when it tried to gain ground on Guinness. This latter brand had made a virtue of being an acquired taste – a euphemism for "difficult to drink". Among non-Guinness drinkers the taste was a barrier to increased consumption and to entering the market. For many, Guinness no longer represented the core values of the market, not squaring with consumers' warm and romantic view of stout. Guinness appeared a bit aloof and pretentious. Many drinkers were "stout wannabes" who aspired to Guinness, but were put off by its taste and intimidating imagery.

By contrast, Murphy's was easier to drink, a more accessible product. This enabled it to be positioned as "the easy-going stout from mythical Ireland". Tapping into such key elements produced a rise in volume in the on-trade (pubs, restaurants, etc.) of 9,000 barrels a month to a total of 14,000, while share of the stout market grew from 11% to 13%. This was mirrored in the off-trade, where the volume increased from under 2,000 barrels a month to nearly 3,000, and volume share rose from 10% to 13%.

LOCATION, LOCATION, LOCATION

Consequently Murphy's benefited from an emotional gap left by Guinness. However, it is not just what opposes a brand which provides the emotional stimulus for success, but also the context that surrounds it, as was the case with Grolsch lager. It had been successful in the UK in the 1980s, but the 1990s were not so kind. From being the fourth-biggest brand in its sector it had fallen to sixteenth, and sales had declined by 41%, while its sector, premium lager, had grown from 26% to 35% of the lager market.

Grolsch was being marginalized by brands such as Stella and Budweiser, which had clear identities built on a sense of heritage and provenance which were felt to be vital in this market. Its point of difference was that it had a distinctive fuller flavour, due to being brewed for a relatively long time. The "brewed longer" story was, however, dull and irrelevant.

So Grolsch looked as though it was at a dead end. The way out was provided not by research, but by reflecting on its Dutch provenance. A good starting point was the belief on the part of the target audience that genuine premium lager originated outside the UK. Added to this were their positive views of the Netherlands, based largely on their perceptions of Amsterdam as a place with a laid-back, easy approach to life. Grolsch extended this attitude to the way they brewed the beer, positioning it as a laid-back Dutch premium lager, brewed longer for a distinctive taste.

This simple emotional twist resulted in on-trade sales volumes increasing by 58.4% and Grolsch's market position rising to ninth. The rate of purchase in the on-trade grew from 26 gallons a month in 2000 to 80.9 gallons in 2002.

Such consumption would probably be fairly typical of university bars, but the universities need to attract students in the first place. Such was the problem facing the University of Dundee, which found it was having to accept one in four of its students at below the standard entry qualification levels. In considering the reasons for people going to university they identified two main strands: the serious side of gaining a qualification and the social aspect. These were combined into the proposition of "serious fun". This resulted in the downward spiral of applications being reversed and a 7.5% increase over the previous year. Within three years the cumulative increase in applications was 42% and the intake of those with below-par qualifications had fallen to just 12%.

DRESSED TO KILL: GIVING THE BRAND A STUNNING EMOTIONAL NUMBER

The solution that the University of Dundee found came from a simple amalgam of the two key elements in the offer presented by universities and, as such, was exploiting generic emotional values. It is also possible, however, to provide a brand with an emotional cloak that then becomes

---

"Serious fun"

---

a key part of its appeal to the consumer. This was achieved by Thomasville furniture in the USA. They had discovered that new furniture tended to be devoid of meaning and emotionally bereft. It was viewed from a utilitarian and styling perspective. Only over time did it begin to be imbued with a patina of meaning. Coupled with this was the fact that men were reluctant furniture shoppers and would accompany their wives out of duty rather than interest.

These two elements gave a basis for what Thomasville called the Ernest Hemingway Collection. This helped make an immediate and emotional connection with the target, especially men, giving the brand a depth it otherwise lacked. The resulting sales of $34 million in the first four months and over $100 million in the first year, made it the largest launch in the company's history.

TURNING PLOUGHSHARES INTO SWORDS: CAPITALIZING ON EMOTIONS WITHIN THE CONSUMER

Thomasville triumphed by taking a rather superficial approach, hijacking the emotional values associated with Ernest Hemingway and wrapping them around their furniture. Yet the spark for an emotional positioning does not necessarily come from the outside, but can emerge from the inner emotions of the consumers – particularly with regard to such a sensitive subject as incontinence pads. Few people want to admit to using these, yet, in Australia, at least one in three women who have had children have a weak bladder.

Tena took this finding and used it as a way of overcoming embarrassment with emotion, by connecting the issue with the positive experience of being a mother. In addition, the fact that one in three women suffered from it showed that it was no big deal and helped women regard it not as something particular to them, but rather something that was widespread. This resulted in total category growth climbing from 5% to 20% and Tena's share of this enlarging market rising from 51.1% to 55.4%.

Motherhood had helped the mother have a more positive image of herself, but her main concern in this role is for her children. One of the ways this manifests itself is through an interest in what they eat and drink – an emotional cord that Kia-Ora orange squash (an orange concentrate which is diluted with water) pulled on in the UK.

They had found that orange was the dominant flavour in the squash market, with 62% of the volume, and that children were the major consumers, with over 60% of the volume accounted for by the 2 to 15-year-old age group. There were some negatives associated with the own-label sector as it was viewed as weak and poor value for money, and concern was expressed as to whether children would like it. By contrast Kia-Ora came out best in blind taste tests. This led to capturing the concept of "the good squash" for the brand. Mothers could be assured that their children would like it and there was reassurance on its content, particularly its fruitiness.

In terms of addressing the mothers directly, this translated into Kia-Ora being "the squash for kids" (as its main competitor – Robinson – was quite adult) and also describing itself as the orangeyest squash. Within two years Kia-Ora went from being third in the market to being half the size of the brand leader, with share increasing from 8.8% to 14.5%.

By the end of this climb it had wrested market leadership for itself. A success achieved by playing on one of the most basic concerns – that of a mother for her children.

The concern over what is eaten and drunk also extended in the UK to red meat, with sensitivity over admitting to its consumption, as the perception of red meat eaters was that they were overweight, old fashioned and unsophisticated. In contrast chicken and fish eaters were seen as controlled, virtuous and contemporary. Also, many consumers were not actively avoiding red meat, but rather saw other meals as more convenient.

The riposte to this scenario was to convey home-cooked red meat as uniquely filling, warming and sustaining. It was portrayed as providing a sense of comfort and well-being – a feeling of being loved and valued. In addition all this was associated with pleasant and convenient eating articulated in the positioning of the "recipe of love".

"BMOC – big man on the campus – laid back and confident"

Another group concerned about its image, but for totally different reasons, is the older teens. Coca-Cola had a citrus carbonated soft drink called Mellow Yello in the USA which faced stiff competition from Pepsi's Mountain Dew and from another Coca-Cola brand called Surge. The older teen group was the core of this market – male high-school seniors. In contrast with its two competitors, Mellow Yello was seen as sweeter, less carbonated and more drinkable – "easier going down". Talking to late teens about these product facts would not, however, appeal to their emotional requirement to be seen as BMOC (big man on the campus) laid back and confident. Tapping into this emotional potential gave rise to the proposition "Mellow Yello – it's smooth" – exploiting the double meaning of smooth. As a result the decline of Mellow Yello was halted and this was followed by two quarters of growth.

LET'S BE FRIENDS

Halifax Bank of Scotland (HBOS) in the UK tapped into a rather simpler emotion in appealing to the consumer – being friendly. To achieve growth for their Halifax arm they needed to focus on current accounts. These had the highest penetration of any banking products and were the most used. They were the gateway to other products – 68% of current account customers with the main four banks also had credit cards with the same bank.

On a purely rational level Halifax was offering a much higher interest on current accounts than the other main banks – 4% as compared to 0.1%. This helped Halifax capitalize on the tendency of consumers to shop around for credit cards and mortgages and, building on this, to present the current account sector as a retail market, rather than a bank. This was crystallized in positioning Halifax as "Britain's leading modern financial services retailer".

It was realized that underpinning this with the value that Halifax offered would not be a sustainable position as competitors could eventually make the same offer. To stake an emotional heartland that others would find difficult to enter, Halifax made a pre-emptive claim to human values. This was articulated in terms of HBOS presenting themselves as "people not bankers", extra emotional value being provided by their being extra friendly. Such a position was motivating and helped differentiate Halifax from the more corporate, image-based competition. The extent of this motivation was shown by a sixfold increase in Halifax's share of current account switching and a 150% increase in sales for the bank; credit card sales went up 215%. In addition this human portrayal of the bank helped give a significant improvement to staff morale.

OPENING THE BOX: TAPPING INTO LATENT EMOTIONS AROUND THE BRAND

Cases have been cited above where the emotional trigger pulled resides in aspects of the consumer; in some cases it is hidden in the brand itself. Kraft Dinner in Canada had for long been the largest grocery brand in the market; it had been a gold standard and almost a rite of passage for all ages, but it was coming under increasing pressure from own-label, leading to a requirement for a greater volume being offered on deal – at lower prices.

It was these historical roots which formed the basis of the strategy that was adopted. The objective was to trigger the latent affection for the brand by showing consumers – both lapsed and current – that Kraft Dinner understood their connections to the brand. This was in contrast to the strategy they had before, which was addressed solely to kids. This was achieved through such factors as the versatility of the product, which had led to individual consumption rituals, its role as a rite of passage and its value as a comfort food.

Pulling on these cords boosted the brand. The proportion of non-promoted sales – where there was a better margin – rose 30% to 60% of volume. Market share increased and shipments were ahead of budget by 8%.

Something of a more frivolous nature is gambling. The British Columbia Lottery Corporation in Canada already had Lotto 6/49, which was category leader but had reached its maturity and was in slow and steady decline. It was seen as predictable and stable by many, while for others it was dull and unmotivating. With this background, they introduced Super 7 to try to restore interest in the large-jackpot game. As it was new, it had few associations, but it also projected the image of being young, risky and edgy.

This profile led to Super 7 being targeted at light and lapsed 6/49 players. They didn't want it to cannibalize 6/49, however, and so gave Super 7 a position diametrically opposed to it. This consisted of Super 7 being portrayed as recapturing the essence of lottery play: frivolous, indulgent fun. With this positioning, the sales of Super 7 increased by 81.5% over twelve months.

TOO MUCH EMOTION CAN SPOIL THE BROTH

Death and disease are areas around which there is emotion aplenty, and the hazards of smoking can readily don this black cloak. Many anti-smoking campaigns in the UK had made the consumer feel victimized, peppered as they were with too many government health warnings. Also these

"Recapturing the essence of lottery play: frivolous, indulgent fun"

messages had, in the past, come from the Health Education Council, and it was decided that the messenger should move beyond being merely a provider of information to becoming rather a provider of actual service, and should communicate this through a brand that was trusted with health and service – the National Health Service (NHS). The messenger became part of the message. The communication was supported by a range of NHS products and services designed to increase the quitters' success rates.

This approach was further developed by a sophisticated division of the different messages, given that there was no single reason for giving up smoking. This was illustrated by the fact that 76% of smokers who claimed they wanted to give up cited a whole variety of reasons. In response to this, a series of triggers were employed to stimulate smokers to take action.

"The messenger became part of the message"

Overall there was one umbrella theme which encompassed the whole exercise and which stimulated over 90% of those attempting to quit. The whole project represented a key principle at the heart of the NHS – health. There was a focus on the health issues and their emotional and physical consequences in order to encourage smokers to seek support. This was further reinforced by new reasons why smokers should turn to the services that were on offer from the NHS. Again the messenger became a part of the message as the effort was coordinated between different advertisers chosen as the most appropriate for particular messages. For instance, there had been success in California by disabusing smokers of some of their beliefs about smoking which had been fostered by the tobacco industry. The vehicle chosen for this message was Cancer Research UK, which agreed to reveal the truth about the industry's "light and mild" deception.

Similarly, in Australia, there had been positive results associated with the shock element in the message "the damage you are doing now". This connected cigarettes with internal organ damage. In the UK this particular aspect was taken up by the British Heart Foundation (BHF), which brought its authority to bear on the link between smoking and the heart. As a further finessing of the message, the BHF set out to be anti-cigarette rather than anti-smoking or anti-smoker – so helping to distance itself from blaming people or their habits and rather attacking an inanimate object. Finally, there had been much evidence amassed in California and Massachusetts on the damage that passive and second-hand smoking could do to those with whom smokers had strong emotional attachments. This banner was raised by the NHS, which was deemed as particularly suitable for an issue whose core was protecting children.

Given the level of sophistication involved in this strategy there was always the possibility that it might have been too complicated and that its overall objective might have been obscured, with the execution of the strategy becoming an end in itself. The ultimate goal, however, was kept firmly in view. The results in moving towards it were impressive. The numbers giving up smoking doubled. The proportion of those who claimed that their giving up was due to being exposed to the advertising strategy rose from 33% to 50% in two years.

The approach of identifying new reasons for giving up also paid off as there was a rise in the number of reasons people put forward for quitting. A particular effort had been made against second-hand smoking. Before, only 28% of respondents had seen it as a health risk to children. Afterwards, it was viewed as the number-one danger, with 56% mentioning it spontaneously. In addition, the percentage of smokers spontaneously expressing concern about heart disease rose from 10% to 21% and extreme concern about clogged arteries from 29% to 45%.

OVERALL

Where the product and the consumer are the two vital elements to be thoroughly considered in the strategy, it is the emotions which provide the bond that will link them. This might be on the most simple and superficial level, as in the "doing something amazing" proposition from the First Citizens bank, or the more rooted theme of friendship employed by the Halifax bank – both pulled on a strong emotional cord and reaped the rewards.

Such basic human themes as friendship are also apparent in the success that Bud Light had in Canada with their understanding of the nature of "guys"; Mellow Yello, with its appreciation of the allure of "smoother" elder teens, and, at the other extreme, the childish traits in adults which Bassett's Liquorice Allsorts managed to tap, offer similar confirmation. Yet there also needs to be awareness of the contribution that factors that might seem to be separate from the brand can make to its emotional link with the consumer. Grolsch possessed a product difference, but this was deemed rather boring, whereas the associations it had with its origin in the Netherlands proved much more fertile ground.

Perhaps the most telling example of the strength of the emotional card was that of Thomasville furniture, which hijacked the emotions associated with Ernest Hemingway and had their greatest launch ever.

4

IF YOU DON'T LIKE THE VIEW – LOOK THROUGH ANOTHER WINDOW

Markets that appear entrenched from one perspective can look ripe from another

Often when people look out over a market they can be rooted to one spot. The view they encounter they imagine to be an accurate image of the field in which they operate. This approach confines their scope for manoeuvre. If they just moved a little they would gain a perspective that could put their efforts into a different framework, one in which the potential for a successful strategy becomes more apparent.

WHEN SIMPLE IS CLEVER

The financial market is one that could never be described as "fun". In the UK in the late 1980s, there was an unprecedented level of activity and publicity in the financial services area, with high-profile flotations of public companies and a resultant popularization of stocks and shares. All this challenged the established perception of finance as being dull and slow moving. This reached the point where many had a nagging suspicion that they were not going with the flow and would be left behind if they didn't make use of the complicated schemes available.

Alliance and Leicester, a building society, met this situation head-on by providing a different perspective, suggesting that if you arranged your finances in a complicated way it could lead to unexpected disasters. They put forward the idea that it was "smart" to be simple. Alliance and Leicester would make your financial life simpler. Their share of receipts increased and became progressively larger than their share of total balances – which would eventually work through to a growth of total balances in the future. In 1986, 6.2% of those with a savings account in the UK had one with the Alliance and Leicester. This leapt to 7.1% by 1991. They were the only building society to achieve market share growth in the period 1986–90 without merging.

WHEN THE NAME OF THE PRODUCT CAN BE A TURN-OFF, FORGET IT

Yet if finance was not viewed as "fun", at least the name of the product was allowed to be. In the case of linoleum, the name itself was a massive negative, which presented a

---

"This led them to avoid telling consumers what the product was"

---

considerable hurdle for Forbo Nairn in the UK when it launched its "Marmoleum" brand, whose name immediately referred consumers back to all the negatives of linoleum. This was despite women liking the product itself.

Forbo Nairn learned, however, that consumers didn't call different categories of resilient floor covering (vinyl, linoleum, etc.) by their correct names. This led them to avoid telling consumers what the product was, focusing rather on the purpose for which it was intended – positioning Marmoleum as a vital ingredient for wonderful-looking contemporary rooms. These were specified as the dining room, halls and conservatories, because they were seen as potential new usage areas. Sitting rooms and bedrooms were unsuited to such a product, and they wanted to steer away from the traditional usage area of the kitchen. The objective was to "own" good looks and practicality. After a successful test market, the brand was rolled out nationally. The total market grew by 6.5%; in the same period the linoleum sector grew tenfold. Marmoleum accounted for 90% of this sector.

This approach of avoiding naming the product, so successfully adopted by Marmoleum, was approached from a different perspective by Qualcast, which ignored the main dynamic of the lawnmower market and latched on to a subsidiary benefit. Qualcast made a cylinder mower that was pitting itself against the hovering Flymo. This competitor was potent in that it provided lightness and total manoeuvrability, making grass-cutting an extension of household cleaning – a sort of garden hoovering. The Concorde cutter from Qualcast was considered by consumers to exceed expectations and do a better job than a hover – cutting closer. Surprisingly it was also felt to be as easy to use and less tiring than the Flymo. This was because it performed the extra task of collecting the clippings as it mowed.

Consequently the task for Qualcast was to make people link the two basic tasks of mowing and raking and so score over the Flymo. This approach also had the benefit of diverting attention from the hover's compelling advantages of lightness, access under bushes and left-to-right movement. It directed the debate towards the seemingly marginal disadvantage of clippings on the grass, which were unsightly and encouraged weeds. Such a change in emphasis boosted Qualcast. The cylinder sector of the market grew by 45% and Concorde increased its sales by 53%. In the second year, the volume leapt a further 9% and the market share reached a record 89%.

WIDENING THE HORIZON

The market view can often be a little restricted. A few paces back can give a better perspective of any extra features that come into play. If the parameters of the market you think you're in feel a bit restricting, you can always look at a wider one.

This was the approach adopted by Throaties in New Zealand. They had only an 8% share and were the fifth-largest brand in the semi-medicated throat lozenge category. The problem they faced was that if people had a really bad sore throat, they thought Throaties were useless, regarding them more as a "lolly". Consequently the best consumers for Throaties to aim at were those who wanted a pleasant placebo to take their mind off the problem. This area, however, was full of the old clichés of itchy sore throats, colds, sniffles and grumpy ill people.

So Throaties widened their horizons by adopting a position in the area of getting the best out of your voice, so differentiating themselves from all the other brands in their market. This was summed up by the line "Throaties speaks volumes". Such an approach spoke volumes in terms of market share, which leapt from 8% to 18% within a year, allowing Throaties to climb to number two in the market. The moving annual total (MAT) of sales changed from −6% to +115% within a year.

This trick of standing back and taking a wider viewpoint was also employed by Vogel's bread in New Zealand. It was the original branded grain bread, but the market had seen a growth in lighter-grain, fresh and specialist breads. This resulted in static sales for Vogel's and reduced profitability, as the consumer had begun to see packaged bread as "a market of sameness", where competition was largely waged through price. The perception of bread was of "earthy nourishment", but Vogel's wanted to widen its approach from "what's best for you" to "pleasurably healthy". This was translated into Vogel's having a certain magic, such that no two people would say the same about it – summarized by the phrase "there's nothing else quite like it".

In terms of the market, the magic worked, with sales rising by 31%, and the frequency of price promotions was reduced from once every four weeks to once every thirteen weeks. Profitability was also addressed by Vogel's average price premium against the standard loaf rising from 28% to 42%, with the price climbing from $NZ1.79 to $NZ1.93.

Vogel's success in expanding the horizons of their product and the role it played for consumers was also mirrored in a very different market – that of ice cream. The Unilever brand Solero faced a problem. It was designed for refreshment, yet ice cream was not perceived by the consumer as offering this – rather it answered the basic physical need of cooling down.

Research throughout Europe had shown that Solero did offer a certain type of refreshment, which was described in terms more normally used to describe drugs and alcohol. In the light of this the Solero experience was put forward as offering a mental lift that left consumers feeling positive, the tangy fruit and creamy ice cream giving a boost and a mind lift. This transferred through to a sales lift, with Solero outperforming the Unilever portfolio growth by 100% and Solero's share of the assortment category of ice cream increasing by as much as 200% in some countries.

CHANGING THE CONSUMER'S VIEW

Whereas Solero managed to settle in a consumer area not associated with ice cream, Bounty kitchen towels' product performance allowed it to stretch the borders of consumers' perceptions of what a kitchen towel offered. Bounty's difference was that it stayed strong when wet, and in order to capitalize on this, consumers had to change the way they used paper towels, no longer thinking of them as just for mopping up spills and liquids.

The position adopted was that "Bounty works when wet, allowing you to handle daily cleaning tasks you never thought a kitchen roll could do". Such a suggestion was enthusiastically taken up, with the cleaning of appliance surfaces rising by 63%, of windows by 76% and the inside of ovens by 285%. To fuel this explosion of uses, Bounty's sales took off, rising from a value share of 9.9% to 16.8% in just six months.

A VIEW THAT'S SO FAMILIAR NO ONE CAN SEE IT

Rather than giving consumers a new perspective, there are often cases where they are so familiar with the view that some aspects are taken for granted and are no longer noticed – like the statues that litter cities and end up being just another piece of street furniture. With the exception of one or two iconic personalities, few know who they depict. Few food items are more familiar than eggs, and we have already seen how in Canada sales of eggs had been languishing before they rose as a result of the marketing proposition "nature doesn't make food that is bad for you", while in contrast other foods tainted by concerns about fat and cholesterol, such as red meat and milk, continued to decline.

At the other end of the world from Canada there was a food that was as versatile as eggs, but which had begun to be viewed in a rather constricted pigeonhole. In Australia, beef mince was seen by mothers as a fall-back meal when they were unsure what to serve for dinner. Usually it was associated only with spaghetti bolognaise. Partly because of this, beef mince was way down on the preference list of children, with only 15% citing it as their favourite meat against 69% for chicken.

This impasse was tackled by suggestions that turned mince from a passive non-think purchase into an actively preferred one. It was recognized that meal times were a high point of activity in a mother's day and a highly stressful situation. Consequently meal solutions had to be quick and easy. Also, mothers were wary of trying new recipes. This led to viewing beef mince as the ingredient for many undervalued dishes that were family favourites, such as meat loaf, meat pie, meatballs and cottage pie. The promise was that children would love all the different meals that could be made with beef mince and that the mothers would love them eating these dishes too. Such love was turned into turnover, with a 16% increase in the weekly consumption of beef mince.

THE BACKGROUND CAN BE JUST AS IMPORTANT AS THE FOREGROUND

One of the key considerations in formulating a strategy is context, and this implies an active consideration of the canvas on which the product is painted rather than just the product itself. Olivio was an olive-oil-based spread which was launched in 1990, but by 1995 it was own-label which was driving sector growth, with a 60:40 ratio to Olivio. The most compelling claim for Olivio was that of reducing cholesterol and improving heart health, but this territory was already taken by Flora, another Unilever brand. It was noted, however, that attitudes to health were changing, and that many now saw it as something that resulted from an overall approach to life rather than a field to be tilled only on certain occasions.

In talking of olive oil, the previous emphasis had been on what it did; now the focus changed to looking at its context, which was Mediterranean. This brought with it a wider significance. There was World Health Organization data that showed a much lower incidence of coronary heart disease in the Mediterranean, combined with longer life expectancy. Consequently Olivio was able to position itself as part of an olive-oil-rich Mediterranean diet which could help you enjoy a longer life. This distanced the brand from Flora, gave some emphasis to real emotion and a soul and some spine to the brand. It also gave it healthy sales, with Olivio's volume increasing by 77% in a year, resulting in a reversal in the ratio of its sales to own-label to 60:40 in Olivio's favour. This was also adopted as an approach for the whole European market, with sales increasing from €40 million in 1997 to around €100 million in 2001.

MOVING ON TO A HIGHER PLANE

Even the most complex and advanced markets can benefit from the occasional expedition to a higher peak so that the view takes in a broader perspective than the fierce hand-to-hand combat that is the everyday struggle for so many products. This was true of the fastest-growing consumer market in history – the mobile phone. When Orange launched in the UK in 1994 it was confronted by a market dominated by Cellnet (now O_2) and Vodafone, both already with ten years' experience behind them. Despite being such a new market, it had quickly descended into confusion, distrust, complicated tariffs, deals and prices. Orange was offering per-second billing and inclusive minutes which would save 20–40% on Cellnet/Vodafone.

"Deliver its price-based message from a position of brand strength and not commodity weakness"

Despite having this clear advantage, however, Orange wanted to secure the high ground of branding unoccupied by the competition, and once this was secure it could then descend into the melee and deliver its price-based message from a position of brand strength and not commodity weakness. It positioned itself as first and not last: first in being wire free and owning the future – summed up in the line "The future's bright. The future's Orange". This distanced it from the vocabulary and associations of the existing market. Eventually this distance was a gap so large that all the competition could see of Orange was dust. Within eight years Orange became the market leader in the UK.

Often when the view changes, so does the context in which the brand operates, and this affects perceptions of the dynamics of the market in which it operates. These aspects are the keystones of any successful and durable strategy. Yet to bring them into play the approach can be deceptively simple – just look at the view through another window and see the change, above all in terms of success.

5

WHY GIVE IT AWAY?

The short-term nature of pricing platforms
and adding value through positioning

Price cuts are in many respects the antithesis of marketing, as they demonstrate a lack of faith by the company in the ability of its product to sell at a price that will give a reasonable return. As such, they undermine the position of the product as a brand and push it down the treacherous road to being a commodity. Seldom is there a solid excuse for such a slide.

A short-term solution to a product not selling is to lower the price. A blinkered focus on share/volume can, however, result in profit becoming an afterthought until the cavalier price-cutter suddenly bumps into the bottom line and, together with his business, is brought to a sickening halt. Price-cutting can represent a failure to look for the inherent properties of a brand which can give it a unique and distinctive cutting edge – the essence and fascination of marketing.

BREAKING OUT OF THE COMMODITY CUL-DE-SAC

There are many markets where price is seen as the first weapon to be grabbed from the armoury. In retailing this approach is often used for good reasons, such as the use of sales to clear end-of-season stock. It is also applied to everyday shopping items, particularly by supermarkets. Low prices will give an impression of competitive pricing for the store as a whole and so lure customers in. It is often only an "impression", as the smaller margins made on the price-cut items are likely to be made up on other brands. These will not have been dragooned into the first line of attack on the consumer, yet are able to bask in the halo effect of competitive pricing given by the price-cut items.

"Price-cutting can represent a failure to look for the inherent properties of a brand which can give it a unique and distinctive cutting edge – the essence and fascination of marketing"

In addition, with supermarkets in particular, there has been the rise of own-label products. These are essentially price-cut goods, yet they are also sold on the quality reassurance that the reputation of the supermarket has built up. The most remarkable rise in reputation is of Tesco in the UK, a supermarket that had its origins as a heavy price discounter. In the late 1970s it started a fierce price war called Operation Checkout. After this last pricing flourish,

Tesco began to aim for the higher, and more profitable, ground of quality. In 1990 it embarked on a "Quest for Quality", improving the products on offer and the quality of the stores. Tesco appreciated that detail is a prime ingredient for quality and implemented 114 initiatives, such as mother-and-baby changing facilities and removal of sweets from checkouts, which gave an impression of Tesco addressing the needs and concerns of customers.

Such attention to detail even extended to the advertising of price cuts. These are usually announced through the equivalent of screaming on the television and the page, with starbursts as the prevailing visual. The overall impression such a presentation gives is cheapness rather than value, in its sense of good quality at a good price. Mindful of this, Tesco advertised price cuts with individual ten-second ads presenting a single item in a witty way, giving more the feeling of a Harrods sale than a trader at a street market stall.

This careful development of the brand has resulted in Tesco leapfrogging the other supermarkets to arrive at a 30% share of the market, compared with around 16% for its closest competitors, and also a position, identified by a recent survey of 30,000 consumers by BrandIndex, as the UK's top brand.

Moving from the specific case of Tesco to supermarkets in general, one of the frequently used arrows in their quiver is the price of bread, which is used as a useful banner for their price credentials. As a regular and basic purchase, it has consistently spearheaded their attack on the consumer's purse, and many suppliers have been forced to subscribe to the policy of Everyday Low Pricing (EDLP).

This was the fate of Hovis bread, along with most other major bread brands. It resulted in consumers paying 10% lower average prices in real terms. Market share rose, but profit declined. Mathematical (regression) analysis showed that Hovis's sales were closely related to the price at which it was sold – being highly elastic – with 93% of Hovis's share of the market attributable to movements in its price.

Given such elasticity, when price is raised it would be expected that volume would plummet. In the first six months of the brand's relaunch, however, the average price of a Great White Loaf rose from 49p to 57p, and yet volume continued to rise. This resulted in a healthy 32% increase in profits – the brand's price elasticity had snapped.

"The brand's price elasticity had snapped"

The key to this turnaround was a move away from just selling on price. This helped consumers feel they were getting something more than cheap bread. Hovis had a long-term association with "goodness", which had been enhanced by previous campaigns and was articulated in the line "Get something good inside". It was used in the advertising and also communicated on the packaging, which featured shots of good, honest everyday food such as baked beans, tomatoes, cucumbers, etc. This holistic approach from the advertising through to the packaging helped ram home the new position to consumers and give them a reason for buying other than price. Hovis had cast aside the tatty robes of a commodity and attracted the consumer with an appearance more tailored to its nature and past.

"Hovis had cast aside the tatty robes of a commodity"

Being the staff of life, bread is prominent in most grocery markets, and in Canada Wonder bread had managed to operate at an average price premium of 15%. The manufacturers needed to maintain and enhance this position, however. To achieve this they built on the universal desire of parents to do what is right for their children and the fact that childhood has lots of ups and downs. Such insights were the foundation for presenting Wonder as part of a complete childhood – a position that helped sales rise by 22%, 20% and 12.5% in 1997, 1998 and 1999.

IT'S NOT JUST THE PRODUCT, BUT WHAT COMES WITH IT

With bread and supermarkets, price cuts are often the default mode, as was the case with car repair chain Kwik-Fit in the UK. They dominated their market of "fast fits" with while-you-wait car part replacements and repairs. But their sales were slipping and little had been invested in marketing. Their knee-jerk response to this was to turn to price cuts. These gave a brief but unsustainable lift in sales. A more considered strategy was required. In research over half of respondents said they would consider Kwik-Fit, but that it wouldn't be the first place they would go. There appeared to be nothing to distinguish it from the competition apart from the blue of its logo. There was a feeling that Kwik-Fit was past it.

The response was to look for focus and, with over 90% of sales coming from tyres and exhausts, they didn't have to look far. In the past, in line with their overall price strategy, Kwik-Fit had focused on budget tyres, which meant they had a lower share in the higher-value branded market. Now they highlighted famous-brand tyres, saying their prices were coming down and staying down. The sales decline reversed.

"They examined the assumption that, in a low-interest market, price was the only thing worth talking about to non-loyalists"

This approach was still talking price, however, albeit at a higher level. This still permitted consumers to believe that Kwik-Fit didn't care about quality, and some consumers were rejecting them on this basis. Such a malaise led Kwik-

Fit to look for a more positive remedy. They examined the assumption that, in a low-interest market, price was the only thing worth talking about to non-loyalists. Previously held beliefs were turned on their heads when the research discovered that most non-loyalists, who accounted for 50% of the market, were not shopping on price but were looking for recommendations, as they wanted quality and honest, reliable service. Also, an enduring truth was that neither sex enjoyed having to organize car repairs, but, because men didn't like admitting to an "unmanly" fear of garages, it was easier to address their fears if they believed that women were being targeted.

The positive experience of Kwik-Fit was heightened by the context of negative expectations with regard to garages. And the positive feelings of consumers translated into positive sales, with profits rising from £43.6 million to £58.8 million in one year. An even greater achievement was that the venture capital company that had bought Kwik-Fit was able to sell it for £800 million, having bought it only three years earlier for £330 million from Ford, who had originally paid around £1,000 million – the swings and roundabouts of astute strategic thinking.

A story that has developed over time is that of Andrex toilet tissue. This is a soft tissue that was launched in the UK back in 1956, when hard tissues had a 75% share. By 1963 it had a 25% volume share. Andrex continued to pursue a policy of quality at a premium price that was 15% over own-label, whereas other competitors had either become own-label or sold on price. Over the years this premium increased to 30% and the brand still managed to sustain a market share of around 30%. It had helped keep the initiative in its market by keeping up with and even anticipating customer requirements: it was the first brand to introduce coloured tissues, it kept up the product quality and built up good grocery distribution (toilet paper having been traditionally sold through chemists).

This can also happen when a brand enters a market in which products tend to be viewed and treated as commodities rather than brands, yet the marketing of the brand takes the bold step of not venturing out on to the thin ice of price. This was the case with Cravendale milk in the UK. They realized that, owing to the costs involved in the unique filtration process they used, in order to be a commercially viable product, they needed to sell at a 28% premium over the price of standard milk. To support this higher price they had tried to position Cravendale by listing the benefits it offered: purity, better taste and longer life.

Although all these competitive advantages were valid, the litany of benefits resulted in a lack of focus which didn't offer consumers a simple reason why they should pay a higher price. The concept was honed down to "the freshest tasting milk" – a clear message which could be exploited both in advertising and promoting the brand. But focus can be extended to areas other than the message. The number of pack sizes was reduced to just the 2-litre size, as this was the volume most appropriate for the principal target – families.

The results were impressive. "The improvement in sales wasn't the result of extra communication spend. It was the result of a more powerful idea," as one of those working for Cravendale stated. The brand achieved a turnover of £41 million and a growth rate of 45% in a year. Such success was accomplished while maintaining the 28% price premium.

IF THE ROOM'S TOO SMALL, GO FOR AN UPGRADE

Occasionally, an increase in volume is not possible because of restrictions imposed from outside the market, as with Anchor butter from New Zealand. The UK's treaty with the European Economic Community imposed a quota on imports of dairy products from New Zealand. A further rein on expansion was a cap on New Zealand's share of the butter market: if it exceeded 30% there would be a review of the quotas.

Fortunately there was some room for manoeuvre as 27% of the New Zealand butter imported was unbranded and sold in bulk. Selling some of this butter under the Anchor brand name and so finding a justification for a higher price would help increase the return. Unfortunately this plan suffered from the major inconvenience that Anchor had been the opposite of a premium product, having been sold at own-label prices or below. An added complication was provided by a decline in overall butter consumption, with butter's share of the yellow fats market (butter, margarine and other spreads) falling from 70% to less than 30% in just five years.

The only area of manoeuvre remaining for New Zealand butter was the product itself. To justify a premium price, Anchor had to demonstrate a perceived advantage over the competition. This was provided by asserting that the milk used to make it was richer and more natural as the cows ate grass all the year round. Such information gave the consumer some justification for the higher price Anchor charged. From 71% of the quota being sold as branded Anchor butter, the branded share rose to 84% within five years.

Anchor butter increased its share of the butter market to the optimum 30% level, slowed down its volume decline and, at the same time, raised its price relative to own-label. That Anchor was able to raise its relative price during this period and increase market share was even more impressive given that this success was in the middle of a recession.

Another brand that was constrained by quota limits was Mazda. It was limited to 1% of the UK car market by a trade agreement. Unfortunately there was also a substantial appreciation of the yen against the pound, from 450 to 220 yen over four years. Consequently the only way to increase turnover was to raise the value of the cars sold by changing the mix to the more expensive models. Mazda found a position for their higher-priced 626 range, based on it coming top in a German road test and being voted by US motoring journalists as the best imported car in the USA. For the 323, the fact that it had more interior space than its competitors was highlighted.

The result of this emphasis was that the mix of the cars sold swung towards the more expensive 626, and the price rises Mazda were able to implement over two years, of 18.2% for the 626 and 16.4% for the 323, were the highest in their respective sectors.

IF EVERYONE ELSE IS DOING IT – ALL THE MORE REASON NOT TO

There are many markets where price-cutting is driven not by the retailers but by competition between the manufacturers themselves. It can even become accepted as one of the rules of engagement in a particular market. This is never due to the particular DNA of such markets, but rather to the attitudes of those who operate within them.

"Much creativity has been involved in the pursuit of more novel and enticing ways of presenting these price cuts instead of devoting energy to avoiding them"

The car industry in Europe and the USA has long been such a battlefield, as overcapacity has led to heavy price-cutting. Indeed, much creativity has been involved in the pursuit of more novel and enticing ways of presenting these price cuts instead of devoting energy to avoiding them. This was particularly noticeable in the summer of 2005, when General Motors in the USA had a "successful" price promotion. It described its prices as being those offered to its employees. The other American manufacturers followed suit – whereas Toyota in the USA announced price *increases*. In 2003 the average profit per vehicle made by Toyota was $2,400, whereas the figure for GM was $300.* Such comparisons help explain why GM was worth $16 billion in 2005 and lost over $10 billion, whereas Toyota had a market capitalization of $160 billion.†

PUTTING A JET UP PRICING

Another example breaking through the received wisdom of the car market was that of Saab in the UK. Their limited production capacity of around 130,000 units a year necessitated finding a profitable niche that could help propel Saab upmarket. They had experienced three years of static sales and their prices, far from moving towards a premium, had been going in the opposite direction, falling behind the Retail Price Index (RPI). Their dealers' profitability was also squeezed by the need to offer large discounts in order to push sales.

Something needed to be found to reverse this sorry state. Rather than looking outside at the market and wondering how it might fight its corner, Saab looked inwards and found

---

* *Financial Times*, 21 July 2004.
† *Guardian*, 27 October 2005.

strengths and unique points about itself that no one had previously noticed. Saab had long manufactured military jets for the Swedish air force. This was a property that research indicated was unique, highly motivating and previously unexplored. On an emotional level, the analogy between a fighter pilot and the driver of a Saab was highly motivating. The claim "the aircraft manufacturer" gave the brand credentials and expressed a personality in a market where advertising constantly tries to invest cars with personalities rather than expressing something already there. Also, it was a position that was related to the marque, not to a specific model. This was significant, as with more expensive cars it tends to be the marque which consumers focus on rather than the model. It was this association which invested Saab with the premium status it required.

The resultant increases in price were impressive and swift and overtook the RPI. In addition the mix of Saab models with better specifications increased, the turbo and injection models moving from 49.4% of sales to 84.6%. Overall turnover rose from £84 million to £144 million in three years (+71%), while profit went up by 331% to £8.2 million over the same period.

EXPENSE CAN COME OUT OF THE CLOSET

In many instances the setting of a price appears to be an area of uncertainty for many manufacturers. Given this attitude it is refreshing to come across brands that have the confidence and sure footing to embrace their price rather than shy away from it. They are proud to be pricey. In the car market, Porsche, which sells on quality and could never be accused of stooping to price, is consistently the most profitable car manufacturer in the world – with profits before tax of €2.1 billion on a turnover of €7.3 billion in 2005/06.

"Proud to be pricey"

On a rather more prosaic level, the use of a higher price has seldom been better illustrated than by Stella Artois beer in the UK, which the Effectiveness Awards termed "more of a case study of an effective brand than effective advertising". The position of Stella in the UK market is extraordinary. One in every four pints of premium lager sold in the on-trade is Stella; it is the biggest-selling lager in the off-trade, is one of the top five grocery brands by value and is the biggest alcoholic brand by value in the country. Not bad for a lager that consumers don't like! In blind taste tests it consistently came bottom, as it was considered too bitter. Also, in its home country of Belgium, it had always been considered as a swilling lager, lacking any premium credentials.

It was not just the product itself which could have held the brand back; the market conditions in the early 1980s when it initiated its long-term position were unpromising. The overall volume of beer sold in the UK was in steady decline.

Consequently it was crucial that margins should be maximized. A premium lager sector had emerged with a product that was a bit stronger than standard lager and delivered a profit of 5p more per pint. Yet Stella chose to position its price at a further premium of 5p above the average for this sector. Of this extra margin, 4p was assigned as profit, the remaining 1p going towards the advertising.

Unlike others in a similar situation, rather than try to hide its premium price, Stella decided to flaunt it. This was on the risky principle that if consumers see something is expensive they often assume it is worth it. From 1982, it made it into an asset with the phrase "reassuringly expensive", used to underwrite the quality of the brand. This was also a good phrase for the trade as it helped persuade the publican that the premium wasn't just a short-term ploy to persuade him to stock Stella, but rather a long-term commitment.

Although this position remained, it was also flexible enough to be interpreted differently in line with the times. During the rather brash 1980s the connotations were those of exclusivity and high price. With the dawn of the 1990s, the overall positioning was able to encompass a move from symbolizing something expensive, along with the ability of the consumer to pay, to a position where it symbolized a lager of supreme quality and worth. Such a shift helped feed the consumer's feeling of discernment as a drinker. Flattery of the consumer is always a seductive way of endearing them to the brand – as is the case in most human relationships.

The appeal that Stella had been able to fashion for itself was summed up in research: "It has a classy and expensive image, but an actual price that is within reach of most people" (Terry O'Brien). Its sales volume went up 406% between 1981 and 1989. From 1991 to 1995, volume grew by 67% in comparison with 16% for the rest of the market. The positioning had given the consumer a point of distinction for the brand, and the salesman had a lever to manipulate the publican into stocking it.

As in the case of Tesco above, the articulation of Stella's position was consistent in every detail. In the 1980s and 1990s in the UK, the default approach for the advertising of lagers was to make the campaigns as wacky as possible to appeal to what was known as the "lads" market, and hope that some of this distinctive eccentricity would rub off on the brand and then transfer to the consumer's self-image. Stella took a totally different approach, more in line with the considered tone of its "reassuring" position, presenting itself through sophisticated advertising with a distinctly French Provençal theme (although the beer is Belgian) derived from the film *Jean de Florette*. This cultural appreciation was further manifested in a careful sponsoring of good-quality movies on television. For most other lagers, culture was something found in a yogurt pot!

TO A PREMIUM AND BEYOND

Making a silk purse out of a pig's ear is not the only approach that can be exploited in terms of successful positionings. For those with a bold streak and a little imagination, there is the challenge of successfully charging an additional premium on a product whose market is already a premium category. Champagne is an icon of luxury and its price reflects this, yet Lanson was able to take this further in the UK.

"For most other lagers, culture was something found in a yogurt pot!"

As with many of the other products discussed above, there is a ceiling to the output of champagne. This is due to nearly all the available land in the Champagne area being under the vine. Consequently the only way to increase turnover is through higher prices, rather than increased volume.

Most champagnes did not advertise, having long been in a seller's market. After some initial false starts, Lanson found a position that distinguished it from the usual clichéd champagne images, but was true to the brand and personal to the consumer. Lanson was presented as being for people to create their own "Champagne Moment". This reflected the special-occasion aspect of champagne, but also flattered the self-image of the consumer – usually a rewarding target for a bit of pandering.

Over five years Lanson outperformed the market by 32%. Market shipments improved by 92%, whereas Lanson's rose by 124%. In addition this was achieved with an increase in prices of 10% against the market. As a result, turnover was £10 million above the projected value.

BUILDING VALUE

"We could double Bowmore's volume by halving the price, but we want to build long-term value" – these were the words of the marketing director of Bowmore, a producer of malt whisky. They sum up a familiar dilemma when tackling a market and show a healthy awareness of the bottom line rather than being seduced by the siren call of volume and share which have enticed so many marketing plans and brands on to the rocks.

"The siren call of volume and share which have enticed so many marketing plans and brands on to the rocks"

Bottled whisky accounted for 44% of Bowmore's volume and 78% of its value. This was because the greater part of its product was sold in bulk as a commodity. At the time, supermarkets were beginning to wield more power in this sector (as they accounted for 64% of sales) and encouraging whisky brands to discount. The two main players in the malt whisky market – Glenfiddich and Glenmorangie – were caving in to these demands and taking money from above the line to fund heavier discounting.

Bowmore's response showed some of the boldness for which Highlanders are famous – they used advertising as leverage to help dissuade retailers from demanding discounts. Taking such a risk needed a strong position which, through assiduous research, they were able to winkle out of the product. As it is a malt from the island of Islay, Bowmore is characterized by a peaty/smoky taste which gives it a more complex character and a more challenging taste than its two main competitors, Glenfiddich and Glenmorangie. These distinctive traits fuelled the proposition "surrender to the adventure" and to an articulation of the Bowmore legend based on folk tales from Islay.

This was the strategic leap that vindicated the marketing director's ambition. In one year the average retail price of Bowmore went up 3%, whereas for the market as a whole there was an average price decrease of 2%. It became the fastest-growing malt in the top ten brands with a volume increase of 36% and an increase in value of 33%. Bowmore was not able to avoid discounting completely, but while the average for the market was £5–6 per bottle, Bowmore managed to get away with just £3.50.

Such awareness of heritage exploited by Bowmore also came to the aid of one of its main competitors – Glenmorangie. They discovered that the name of the brand in Gaelic meant "the Glen of Tranquillity". Although tranquillity was recognized as a generic property of whisky, Glenmorangie laid claim to it with its connotations of relaxation and quiet reflection combined with the functional benefit of purity.

In the first year sales increased by 18% in volume and 13% in value, while in the most dynamic sector, the multiples, volume increased by 27%. These increases were not, however, at the expense of the bottom line, as the second year of this new positioning saw Glenmorangie achieve an increase in its price premium over the sector of 56%, which was largely due to an increase in the sales of its more expensive malts.

BEEN AROUND FOR A WHILE – MAYBE IT'S TIME FOR A MAKEOVER?

There are many brands that seem to be an integral part of a market, such that their absence seems inconceivable – like trying to imagine Paris without the Eiffel Tower or New York without the Empire State Building. This may be a reassuring picture for the consumer, but it can be a seductive one for those charged with responsibility for the brand.

Such was the case with Rimmel, a well-established UK cosmetics company, which was the entry point into this market for many teenage girls. Continued high volume had, however, hidden an erosion of profitability. Rimmel's price was below that of the mass-market average. They wanted to close this gap in price without losing the good-value positioning that was still felt to be essential for the brand's success.

Rimmel discovered that London held a special position in the minds of their target market. It represented an edgy, experimental interpretation of beauty, not the pretentious, perfect look promised in most cosmetic advertising. This led to the positioning of Rimmel as "Beauty made in London", personified by the model Kate Moss.

Net sales increased by 21% and profits by 25%. In terms of prices, they had risen 14% against the previous year and 29% against the level two years before. The average unit price had risen from £2.38 to £3.09 over two years.

OVERALL

It is not necessarily the inherent attributes of a brand which enable it to charge a premium. Rather it is the focus that is given to aspects which are felt to resonate with the consumer. It is these which instil a set of beliefs that persuade the consumers that the premium price they are paying is worth it. The only thing that really matters from the point of view of marketing is perception. It is perception which creates value, and nothing else.

Stella Artois did not change its nature over the years. It was still the premium lager that came bottom in blind taste tests, yet it managed to charge a premium and become brand leader. Despite having a few initial hiccups, Cravendale was able to refine its position and propel itself to success. Even among brands in markets already regarded as having premium prices, such as Lanson, Glenmorangie and Bowmore, there is still the potential to make that premium greater.

In addition, there are occasions when premium pricing is pursued not just for its own sake, but as a response to a particular market situation. This was the case with Mazda, which had an agreement not to increase volume, and Anchor butter, which was subject to a similar constraint through trade treaties. For both there was a simple solution to the dilemma of not being able to sell more – make more (money), through selling at a higher price.

As discussed, price cuts are in many respects the antithesis of marketing. Seldom is there a solid excuse for a brand's slide down the treacherous slope to being a commodity. This was illustrated by the case of Hovis bread, which was in one of the tightest price straitjackets of any product category, yet managed to break out. All that is required is some thought and common sense.

6

JUST LOOK IN THE MIRROR

Looking at a brand the other way round can turn it right side up

Often the perceived elements within a market can take on the status of rigid rails along which it is assumed that any strategic journey should travel. Such a blinkered outlook overlooks the dynamic tension of many markets and the ever-present possibility of turning a problem on its head.

MAKING BLACK WHITE

There are few more extreme examples of this than Sunlight Laundry detergent in Canada, which, instead of focusing on cleaning, turned its attention to getting dirty. It was a distant number-two brand in the market whose share had fallen to 13%, dwarfed by Tide's 46%. In the consumers' minds Tide owned "clean" – so where could another detergent go? The path that opened up was a dirty one.

Sunlight subscribed to the regular belief in realizing that dirty clothes are a drag; they then took a large leap, however, in recognizing that activities which get clothes dirty can be fun. So they came up with the proposition that Sunlight allowed you to get as dirty as you liked because it would then clean your clothes. Just as Tide owned "clean", so Sunlight took possession of the other end of the spectrum – "dirt" – with the line "Go ahead, get dirty".

"Go ahead, get dirty"

As with any clear, distinctive and simple strategy, Sunlight's position enabled focus to be given to activities in areas other than advertising. They sponsored events where there was lots of dirt and people having fun, such as the Calgary Stampede, local rodeos and the Canadian mountain bike circuit. The result of all this was that the brand shifted up a few gears. In the first year its share increased by 28% and in the second by 8% – all at the expense of Tide.

FINDING ANOTHER DIMENSION TO THE BRAND

Yet the position of Sunlight had been nowhere near the grim prospect facing Polaroid in the UK. The brand had lost its relevance, the cost gap with 35mm cameras had widened from twice to nearly six times more expensive, and the competition had also improved by being simpler and smaller. Polaroid had brought out the Vision, which measured up to the 35mms' technical standards, but there was no improvement in sales.

So, like Sunlight, Polaroid looked though the other end of the telescope. They found that when people posed for 35mm photos they tended to be stiff and formal while, when a Polaroid was being used, they would be more expressive and sociable – the instant nature of the camera encouraged people to let their hair down. This led to a realization that Polaroid was not a camera like Canon, Nikon and Minolta, but rather a social lubricant like Bacardi and Coke. It gave people the opportunity to live life on the edge, a point expressed in the proposition "live for the moment". There was nothing momentary about the increase in sales, with cameras going up 91% and film by 46%.

MOVING THE GOALPOSTS

Just as Polaroid changed the way their cameras could be seen, so Mazola in the UK extended the perception of its role within the kitchen. Mazola was operating in a market where two-thirds of the volume went to own-label and where much of the growth had come from deep frying, a role for which it was ill placed as this was commodity based. Although deep frying was the dominant factor in the market, there was evidence that this position was changing and also, despite the obvious volume requirements of deep frying, the proportion of those who deep fried was smaller than that of those using oil for other jobs, such as shallow frying, roasting, grilling and baking.

This led to Mazola setting up a spectrum of usage from deep frying at one end to salads at the other. Research indicated that, moving along this axis, two factors became of increasing importance: the taste of the oil, and concern about what it was and where it came from, including an implied interest in healthy eating. This led to describing Mazola as "100% Corn Oil". The key aim in this description was to convey purity, which played a minor role in deep frying, but was crucial in salads. It immediately differentiated Mazola from its cheaper competitors such as Crisp 'n Dry by moving the playing field to a pitch where Mazola had a competitive edge and could add value by attaching important emotional reassurance. This resulted in a gap between it and the competition in market share as well. Where this positioning was implemented, Mazola's share grew by 12%, whereas it declined by 12% in those parts of the country not using it. Further underwriting this growth was a reversal in the decline of Mazola's penetration.

STUFF BEING SERIOUS – HAVE FUN!

The purity message of Mazola paid dividends. In the case of Vita-Wheat in Australia, however, it had to look beyond the integrity of the product and interpret it in a more compelling way for the consumer. Its claim that it was "made from 100% natural ingredients" was strong, but it had been experiencing two years of continuously declining sales. Ryvita and other crispbreads occupied the rather austere world of diet and control, giving no hint of enjoying life. Recognizing this, Vita-Wheat adopted a "want to" position as opposed to the "have to" approach of Ryvita. This was expressed in the phrase "Vita-Wheat gives me the vitality to live life to the full" – a positive message, which translated into positive sales with growth of 22% after a previous decline of 21%.

WHEN THE BASIC BENEFIT IS TOO SERIOUS, ADD A LITTLE GLOSS

Vogel's grain bread may have looked different to each person who looked in the mirror, as we saw earlier, but to most people Kellogg's Bran Flakes appeared the same, and what they saw they weren't too keen on. It was only on looking closer that aspects were spotted which few had noticed. Bran cereals had remained a minority-appeal product with consumer attitudes being largely negative; many consumers were not even prepared to try them. Forty years of presenting All-Bran as "Nature's Laxative" had hardly helped the cause. Despite this they felt that Bran Flakes had the potential for greater general appeal as a cereal.

"Vita-Wheat adopted a 'want to' position as opposed to the 'have to' approach of Ryvita"

They gave consumers samples of the standard product in blank packs to take home. Their response was that it was delicious, and many refused to believe they were Bran Flakes, as their image of bran was of something bought primarily for its medicinal and health qualities and not for taste. This led Kellogg's to give Bran Flakes a little gloss by concentrating on the tastiness of the product and leaving it to the word "bran" to provide the health reassurance. Ironically this proved doubly fortuitous, as it was at this moment that a diet book called *The F Plan* came out, which proved to be very popular. It put great emphasis on high-fibre foods, and Bran Flakes was ideally placed to provide this. Because it tasted good, the usual hair-shirt connotations of bran could be avoided. Its sales rose by 41%, even though it had been in marginal decline the year before, while the bran market as a whole grew by 37%. The following year Bran Flakes grew by a further 23%, whereas the sector as a whole slowed to just 9% growth.

CONTINUOUS IS MORE THAN OCCASIONAL

A similar move from serious to more appealing was achieved by Lucozade, a glucose-based drink, in the UK. This was a brand that had been linked to illness and convalescence, positioned as a unique source of liquid energy that helped the family when recovering from sickness, for kids and occasional usage only. This base was shrinking, however, as Department of Health figures indicated that there were fewer flu epidemics and less illness generally. In addition, hard times and inflation had led to an increase in cynicism with regard to paramedical products – a situation not helped by Lucozade's price consistently rising above the rate of inflation. With this and the fall in marketing support, sales declined.

But the background to Lucozade's position had some rich
pickings. A need was identified for a pick-me-up for
housewives during the day. This led to repositioning it as a
unique source of energy when healthy as well as when sick,
changing it from an occasional purchase into a regular one.
Rather than being positioned for an emergency, Lucozade
adopted the more subtle approach of being a continuous aid
to the maintenance of health, claiming to help the body
regain its normal energy levels. This had the result of
transforming the previous decline into a rise in volume sales
of 13%.

"Rather than being positioned for an emergency,
Lucozade adopted the more subtle approach of being a
continuous aid to the maintenance of health"

Taking a particular perception and pouncing on its mirror
image proved to be a great springboard for BT, the main
telephone company in the UK. Although previous initiatives
had some success in prompting calls, they had done little to
change underlying negative attitudes, which restricted
calling levels. There was little emphasis given to promoting
the positive value of phone communication. Such a product
plus was already well demonstrated by women's use of
phones, as they tended to spend more time on them just
chatting, viewing the pleasure this can give as an end in
itself. In contrast, men would look at a phone call more as a
means to an end, as a functional instrument for delivering a

rational message. This viewpoint would also have some bearing on calls made by women, as men tended to act as the gatekeepers.

Consequently the task was to turn around the perception that women had and persuade men of its validity, in addition answering the anxieties men might have as gatekeepers. BT wanted to reduce price perceptions, as most consumers overestimated the cost of a call by about 40%. This led to the proposition "it's good to talk", as well as highlighting the actual cost of calls by expressing them in terms of everyday purchases – such as a pint of beer. Econometric analysis identified an increased turnover of £297 million thanks to this approach, almost all of which was incremental profit.

DON'T SIT ON YOUR LAURELS, YOU MIGHT NOT GET UP

The pressure on Mazola was a good spur to action; dominance of a market can, however, often act as a comfortable pillow for complacency. Hellmann's mayonnaise in the UK had a 60% share of a market that had been growing for years at 10–20% p.a. In an admirable example of healthy aggression, the Boston Consulting Group picked on Hellmann's not as a cash cow, which its dominance could have suggested, but rather as a prime candidate for investment.

Tall as the tower that Hellmann's had built was, its base was narrow – the product being focused almost exclusively on use as a salad dressing. When it had been launched in the UK this had been its base for operations against a local product called "Salad Cream", and Hellmann's gained a lot of mileage through emphasizing its "real" nature in contrast with the rather ersatz Salad Cream. Although successful, this had left it in a situation where most were buying it *in addition* to Salad Cream and using it on special occasions only.

Faced with this scenario, Hellmann's needed to re-present itself as a brand with a wider range of uses and divorce itself from the seasonality associated with salads, making consumers see it as a versatile condiment. Such a move had greater potential for growth. Curiously many of the heavier users of Hellmann's were already using it in a variety of different ways, but such was the pedestal on which the brand had been placed that many of them were embarrassed by such usage, regarding it as not "proper" – almost sacrilegious. Such usage was in line with current trends, however, as there was a rise in snacking and a decline in formal dining. So Hellmann's was positioned as though it were a new product, redefining it as a versatile condiment/ingredient and cutting it free from any baggage that connected it to Salad Cream. Following this unshackling, Hellmann's flew, with ex-factory sales climbing by 56% in a year.

EASY DOES IT

In managing to blow away the guilty mist that surrounded its extended use by consumers, Hellmann's had emerged into bright sunshine. Another example of looking at a situation the other way round was provided by a sports lottery game, Pro-Line, in Canada. It had reached a peak, but had then slowly declined, a decline that then quickened in pace to 20% in only one year – fewer people were buying tickets. The current players of the lottery knew their sports and saw lotteries as a game of skill, whereas non-players were not very knowledgeable and were not prepared to spend time and energy to get the required knowledge; consequently they were intimidated by lotteries.

In adopting a new strategy Pro-Line looked at the situation from the other side and came to the conclusion that sport was so unpredictable that winning did not in fact depend on knowledge or skill; rather it was a game of chance. This very unpredictability meant that extensive knowledge was not required to win, and the resistance of non-players was overcome with the proposition "because anything can happen, anyone can win". With this approach Pro-Line won, with sales rising 13% over the first six months as against the previous year, and sales for the first fiscal year rising by 15%.

OVERALL

It is easy to assume the general approach that is the common currency of any situation, and the idea of looking at it the other way round can seem perverse, somehow upsetting what is assumed to be the natural order of things. Anyone proposing it is likely to be viewed with disquiet, which is why the courage of those such as Sunlight is to be applauded. Not for their bravery, but rather for their success.

The mirror image of the markets in which brands such as Vita-Wheat and Vogel's operated was fun. To many this may have seemed too frivolous for such prosaic and basic items, yet responding to it put some bubbles in their sales. Just as Polaroid associated a relaxed informality with taking pictures and changed the perception of its role from that of a conventional camera to that of a social lubricant.

At a simple level Lucozade changed its role from emergency aid (i.e. occasional) to that of helping to prevent emergencies happening in the first place – a continuous role. In all these cases it is clear that looking down the other end of the marketing telescope does not necessarily make the solution appear farther away, but rather brings it closer.

7

IS THAT A GENERIC YOU DROPPED?

If **a generic** hasn't been picked up, grab it

One of the most satisfying strategic manoeuvres is grabbing a generic property of the market in which a brand operates and claiming it, so it becomes an integral part of what is perceived as a brand's unique position. It is the perfect pre-emptive strike as, once made, no other brand can claim it without appearing to copy – as in legal matters, "possession is nine-tenths of the law". It has all the appeal and elegance of a skilful move at chess, which checks the opposition with a move that was staring them in the face – if only they had had the wit to recognize it first.

"It is has all the appeal and elegance of a skilful move at chess"

Sometimes the claiming of a generic requires a little finesse, even in such a prosaic market as instant noodles in the UK. Batchelors Super Noodles were stuck with their association with traditional kids' teatime usage. But they had discovered a small group of young adult users who made up for their relatively small numbers by the quantities they consumed.

For them, "filling up" was at a premium, and Super Noodles were seen as quick, satisfying and moreish.

This segment of the market was called "the substantial snacking sector", but the consumers themselves called their purchases "foody nosh". Consequently Batchelors chose to own the term, although it was open to all, being a characteristic of every product on the market, by using the description "great foody nosh" for their Super Noodles. Weekly sales during the advertising of this position rose by 72% and production couldn't keep up with the demand. Also Super Noodles' overall share of the market rose from around 59–65% to 77% with the first burst of advertising and 84% with the second. With such a dominant position in the market there was also an increase in its overall size of 14%.

GETTING UP CLOSE AND PERSONAL

Super Noodles was building on a position of dominance, while in Australia Listerine mouthwash was trying to recover past glories. It had been the first mouthwash and initially had the whole category to itself, but had subsequently slid to a market share low of 23.6%. It had the further negative of an unpleasant strong taste which was felt to be too much for consumers' needs.

This led to Listerine claiming that all mouthwashes freshened breath, but only Listerine killed the germs that caused bad breath and other oral problems. Sales doubled in three and a half years and profits rose by 80%.

... OR JUST VERY PERSONAL

Another product with a personal aspect is women's sanitary towels. Procter & Gamble (P&G) had Always, the most successful femcare brand in the world, with a global worth of over $2 billion and over 50% of the market in many countries. It dominated the developed markets, but in emerging ones its premium position limited its potential, as these were markets where the cheaper brands dominated. To address this situation P&G had launched an inexpensive soft pad called Always Classic, which tested well against competition. The company failed to achieve a satisfactory market share, however, and suffered from the additional problem that a significant proportion of its sales came from other Always variants.

In response to this P&G decided to develop a new brand. The basis of the company's marketing had historically involved establishing a significant product advantage for its brands. Commercial analysis established that for this new brand there was an investment ceiling above which they could not rise, thus precluding any significant advantage. Also, there was a price floor below which they couldn't fall, so preventing any possibility of fighting on price.

Faced with this dilemma P&G went to the consumer for help, conducting some research. This revealed a distinction between the Always consumer and those loyal to mass-market brands. It revolved around a difference between progressive and traditional. The latter group were drawn to what they saw as natural products, and tended to view Always as "technologically plasticky". The thicker pads that the mass-market products used had a plus in that they used cotton in the top sheets. This conveyed naturalness and tradition and the softness of the pads had strong associations with femininity.

This research revealed the latent strength of the whole soft pads category, which had always been present, only no one had spotted it. The nature of the pads reflected the traditional women's preference for things natural and feminine. It remained for Procter & Gamble to claim this territory of "Natural Feminine Care" for themselves, which they did by adopting the name "Naturella" for the brand. This was a unique position in the category and avoided the rational battleground of "value and reliability" or "technological protection".

"Traditional women to whom Naturella appealed saw it as part of the 'gift of fertility', a common euphemism for periods being 'Mother Nature's gift'"

The ground that Naturella occupied transcended the traditional topography of the market, which had been presented as a rational domain where periods were portrayed as a problem, menstruation being just another bodily function. The traditional women to whom Naturella appealed, however, saw it as part of the "gift of fertility", a common euphemism for periods being "Mother Nature's gift". Nature was seen as a timeless, sensual and beautiful thing – a powerful metaphor for protection. Following on from this the "Naturella World of Protection" was seen as somewhere women could feel protected, happy and liberated and could celebrate "what it meant to be a woman".

In countries as diverse as Mexico, Venezuela, Russia and Poland this capitalizing on a generic emotional property by Naturella led to a rise in volume share from 24% to 40% in just three years. An added bonus was that the predicted rate of cannibalization from Always, based on its market share, was 22%, yet such was the distinctiveness of Naturella's position that it took only 15%. All this was achieved despite Naturella having a 5.2% price premium against competitive thick pads.

Naturella resolved a personal problem while Aeroguard in Australia combated something that was up close and personal – mosquitoes. It was market leader with a 51.5% value share, but it was declining slightly, by around 1%. They needed to target all outdoor Australians; it was they who wanted a "mossie-shield". All that was available to Aeroguard was the generic category property of efficacy, so they had to find an engaging way of defining it as unique to Aeroguard. This they did with the concept of a "comfort zone" around an Aeroguard user, where they would be free of annoyance or bother. The comfort for the brand was immediate; over the first three months of the "pest season" value share shot up from 51.5% to 57.6% and volume rose from 49.3% to 54.5%.

SWEET MEMORIES

While Aeroguard prospered by promising protection against annoyance, Ving Tours in Sweden prospered by laying claim to the pleasure people found in the memories of their holiday. It was Scandinavia's largest travel company, with 30% of the market. This very size, however, left it vulnerable to its next-biggest competitor. Its rational point of difference as Scandinavia's largest company for charter holidays with high perceived quality and good value for money had become a given and had no dynamic emotional appeal.

This led Ving to highlight the proposition that, with their holidays, the quality was such that "the feeling lasts longer" after the holidaymaker returned home. This emotional approach leapfrogged over their rational strengths and recovered the lead they had lost to their main competitor.

SELLING THIN AIR

While Ving had claimed the afterglow of a holiday as their territory, Ford captured thin air when launching the Galaxy MPV. They noticed that empty space was valued by people because it made them feel important and special. The Galaxy was regarded as having a lot of empty space, in common with other MPVs. So Ford translated the concept of the luxury of empty space into the proposition "travel first class".

This resulted in a notable upgrade in sales from the initial launch objective – to beat the sales of the Renault Espace, which, at the time, accounted for 50% of the market. The Espace's sales had been running at 7,500 units, whereas the Galaxy dwarfed them with 16,656 units. In addition, Volkswagen launched an almost identical car to the Galaxy, made on the same production line in Portugal, called the Sharan, which achieved sales of only 5,575 units. The power of the Galaxy position was further demonstrated by it being launched at the same time as the Sharan in Germany and France, but without the UK positioning. Taking the average sales of the Galaxy in these two countries as a base for the level of sales in the UK, it was exceeded by 9,197 units.

IF IT DIES IT MUST BE BORN: TURNING "SELL BY" DATES AROUND

Much as the conjuror diverts attention when performing a trick, so can a strategy change the way consumers consider the brand, even altering the criteria by which they judge it. Frito-Lay in Canada made the market leader in potato chips (crisps), Hostess, and another brand called Ruffles, leaving little leeway for a third brand. It had been decided at a corporate level, however, to make Lay's Potato Chips a global brand. In Canada it was a weak old brand which Frito-Lay had sold and then had to buy back. It was promoted on irresistibility with the line "bet you can't just eat one".

Through research it was established that freshness was regarded as a signal of quality, with 65% of consumers rating it as "very important". They thought chips were fresh so long as they were sold within the sell-by date. Lay's took this a step farther by changing the consumers' reference point from "sell by" to "made on", thus giving solid credentials to justify their superior and "irresistible" taste.

And resist the consumers couldn't. Lay's share had been at 29% of Hostess's, but, with the implementation of the new strategy, it shot to 47% above the Hostess share and, within another six months, it dwarfed Hostess with a 111% greater share. This resulted in a doubling of Lay's sales. The strength of such a solid idea, and its adaptability from one market to another, has been underlined by the biggest beer in the world, Budweiser, focusing on the "born on" statement as one of the central planks of its positioning and packaging.

OVERALL

There is a great irony that so much of the emphasis in strategic development has been on making a point of difference for the brand, either in terms of function or emotions. The adoption of a generic bypasses this whole process. In retrospect the generic itself might often appear as an obvious solution, but the fact that no competitive brand had adopted it before makes the adoption of a generic all the more daring and insightful.

This is particularly true of a company like Procter & Gamble, who arrived at their position of being the biggest marketing company in the world by a clear philosophy of creating a product difference and then telling the consumer about it. Yet with Naturella they had the vision to appreciate that this keystone in their corporate culture could be bypassed, and their daring was rewarded. In the high-promotion world of car advertising, Ford was able to realize that the unused space that was common to all MPVs could make a difference. It propelled the sales of the Galaxy far beyond their projections in the UK and the sales the vehicle managed to achieve in other countries. Aeroguard performed a similar trick with their naming of the "comfort zone" of protection from mosquitoes.

The one point to note in all these generic strategies, however, is that not only did they identify the generic that could be claimed, but they then claimed it by presenting it in a way that consumers would view as unique to their particular brand. It is the combination of these two elements which makes for the successful and lucrative exploitation of a generic.

8

NOT BEING ME TOO,
EVEN IF YOU ARE

Establishing a point of difference and
realizing that not always the best product wins
as a brand

One of the recurrent mantras of marketing is to find a point of difference and exploit it. This was enshrined in the philosophies of companies such as Procter & Gamble (for long the biggest advertiser in the world), who would establish a product advantage and then hammer away at the consumer with it.

Many brands have been faced with situations where they have not been able to afford the research to produce such an advantage, or are in markets where the competing brands are, to all intents and purposes, the same. Often the less enlightened would view this as a situation for which the only cutting edge is price competition and so condemn their category and its products to the black hole of a commodity market.

There is always one product advantage that can be exploited, however – this is the determination of those responsible for the brand not to go down the price route and to use their craft and imagination to find a point of difference which, however ethereal, has some meaning for the consumer – the only hook that's worthwhile.

WASHING OR WALKING

Washing hands would not seem the most competitive platform, yet the twist that Carex in the UK gave to this most basic of activities helped revive its sales. There was irony in the adoption of such a route, as Carex had been built on the distinctive product feature of being an antibacterial hand wash. This platform it had used with success, but, after ten years, it was beginning to lose its efficacy – the antibacterial claim had been annexed by household cleaning products and had begun to have harsh connotations.

In the face of this erosion of their product advantage, many manufacturers would focus their efforts on trying to find a new product advantage to leapfrog their previous position. Carex took the opposite approach, and, instead of looking at the product, they looked at the consumer. They established that people who used Carex wanted reliably clean hands. This led them to focus not on the antibacterial angle but rather on the role the product played in people's lives – answering their everyday washing needs. It was the only brand in the liquid soap market not launched on the back of a bigger personal washing brand. This allowed them to claim that Carex knew about cleaning and to concentrate on hands as this would be credible, ownable and would appeal to a wider audience than the core of the brand's current users, and move it away from the kitchen.

This move was made not by stating the attributes the brand offered, but rather broadening its appeal by outlining its role. To achieve this, the biggest hand-washing opportunity was identified as after a visit to the toilet, but there was the difficulty of delivering a harsh message in an emotionally engaging way. This was resolved by the phrase "are you a washer or a walker?", which neatly summed up the situation. Such engagement with a simple process produced impressive results. Penetration of the brand increased, with 300,000 more households buying it than before, and the average weight of purchase went up as well, resulting in a 17.1% increase in the brand's value share. Also, loyalty increased by an impressive 72.2%.

GET REAL, GET TO THE ROOTS

All this was achieved by a simple move from "attribute" to "role". Such emphasis on role can also emerge from a focus on the true nature of the category, as was the case with the Nissan Xterra in the USA. The situation was grim. Nissan was not healthy as a company or as a brand. In the SUV category the competition was fierce, and Nissan's credibility had evaporated. Also, in the particular case of the Xterra, it didn't seem to be so different from the Pathfinder, the model it was replacing.

In looking at the market it was realized that most SUVs were either too small to be practical as SUVs, or too big and so beyond the reach of most people. Transcending this was the essence of a SUV – that it was a vehicle that could take you anywhere. Nissan decided to go back to these roots. They identified a target of men and women aged 25–34 who wanted new SUVs but couldn't afford them and were instead buying used SUVs or pick-up trucks. They didn't want SUVs of the kind that had been taken over by yuppies and soccer moms, they didn't want something associated with middle-aged housewives from Des Moines. Unlike other SUV drivers they didn't go off-road as a goal in itself – as a way of getting a bit of "real" mud on the car and reassuring themselves that the SUV wasn't just a glorified toy. No, they went off-road to do the things they loved, they were real outdoor people. The position of the Xterra in relation to them was summed up in the proposition "everything you need, nothing you don't".

This was based on the functional features and accessories of the Xterra, such as a tubular-style roof rack with a gear basket and other options. Most SUVs had them, but Xterra used them to make the overall position for the car tangible, credible and unique. The credibility was endorsed by the reaction of consumers. Nissan's share of the SUV market rose from 4.3% to 8.9%.

A similar situation faced Isuzu in Canada. They had experienced three years of flagging sales and were being squeezed by the entry of luxury car companies into the SUV market. Isuzu noted that those who considered buying Isuzus or already owned them displayed strong tendencies to want to be seen as different, unusual and not run of the mill. They were sceptical about the arrival of the luxury car companies in the SUV market.

Part of Isuzu's appeal was that they made only SUVs, which led to Isuzu positioning themselves as a specialist who understood SUV drivers and their needs better than any other manufacturers – articulated by the proposition "if you want a real SUV, buy an Isuzu". The three-year decline was reversed and sales grew by 11.3% in a year.

FIGHTING WITH FOCUS

Isuzu showed that focus is important, not just as regards the direction of a strategy, but also in terms of the actual view that is given to the consumer. This was a simple point that was also spotted by Burger King in Quebec. They had only 30 outlets in the province, compared with McDonald's 125, each of which achieved an average of double the sales per restaurant of the Burger King outlets. In addition, McDonald's were expanding their offering to include items such as pizzas and fajitas to reinforce their "something for everyone" positioning. Burger King didn't have the resources to compete across this spectrum, but they wanted to create a unique fast-food identity.

Fortunately their limitation turned out to be their strength. Research showed that consumers preferred the grilled taste of beef and condiments in the Whopper to the Big Mac. So they set out to be Quebec's hamburger fast-food specialist. This was focus enough; after declining sales of 10% a year, they rose 7% and profit went up 4%. By the second year they were breaking all records for Burger King with sales advancing a further 11%. By the third year they had registered growth of 6.3% and had climbed to number two in the market.

OVERALL

Sometimes those trying to develop a strategy can look around desperately for a point of difference that they can pounce upon. They don't realize that it's up to them to make a difference in the way the brand is presented to consumers, rather than searching in vain for something inherent to the product.

When they meet this challenge, as in the case of Carex, where a previous product advantage had to be ditched, the rewards can be great. Even in the case of Burger King, the focus on one tree in the wood as opposed McDonald's obsession with the forest helped them to grow that tree to the towering height of a redwood.

At the end of the day the blunt truth is that is doesn't actually matter whether there is an actual difference or not;

the most important point is that in the perceptions of consumers a seed has been planted from which such a belief grows.

9

CRISIS, WHAT CRISIS?

At no time is clear strategic thinking more important than in a crisis

Fighting to keep or gain market share can be stressful enough, and often requires mobilization of all the resources at a brand's disposal. Such efforts may appear academic when the brand is confronted with a real crisis. This is the time when a clear strategic direction is vital, giving focus to the resolution of the problem and allowing no room for people running around like headless chickens.

Panic might understandably have been the first reaction that greeted the largest and deadliest E. coli outbreak in Jack in the Box restaurants in Washington state in the USA. It was certainly the emotion that predominated in the stock market – the company's shares fell from $17 to $3 and sales in the first quarter after the outbreak fell by 28%. Bankruptcy appeared to be just around the corner.

Their first step was to initiate food quality improvements with visible changes such as "assemble to order" preparation of food. In addition they focused on their core products, which had high perceived quality, rather than clouding the picture with new products. Also, the Jack character was no longer used as just a mascot, but rather as an agent of change. They projected the corporate boardroom as a symbol of business as usual and had Jack blow it up to show that things were going to be different.

And they were. Within three months, sales per store had recovered 50% of the loss suffered due to the crisis. But they didn't stop there; the sales recovery continued for seven years with an industry-leading annual growth rate of 6.6%. The share price rose to $28.25, well in excess of its position before the crisis.

UNITED THEY STAND

Even Jack in the Box didn't experience the death and destruction visited on the Thredbo ski resort in Australia. There was an avalanche that demolished two lodges with the loss of eighteen lives. The media was full of it. The crisis management team that was formed was acutely aware of the approach of the media and forecast accurately how their coverage would evolve: from the initial tragedy, to rescue, victims, reasons, blame and the consequences. A community group of leading citizens agreed to principles and strategies for all communications and to cooperate fully in presenting these in a coherent way to the outside world – the company, village and community needed to speak with one voice.

A result of this unity of purpose was an open letter with a declaration of appreciation to the rescue workers and an expression of gratitude to the Australian public for their sympathy and support. In addition the letter served as a vehicle to launch the Thredbo Family Relief Fund, which had a toll-free number to allow the public to make comments or ask questions.

Although the number of skier days fell 46% in the week after the landslide there was the simple fact that the coming summer season had no connection with the winter tragedy. In promoting this season it was agreed to make no mention of any safety issues that could possibly reignite concerns rather than defuse them. They positioned the resort as a fun alternative to the beach, with the emphasis on fun. The public responded, and summer revenue was up 4% over the previous year. The following winter, however, there was the poorest snowfall for fifteen years, and Thredbo was apprehensive, as it usually suffered more than its major competitors from poor snowfall because the bottom half of its slopes was unusable. In the face of this, Thredbo still managed to grow their market, albeit by 1%.

DECISIVE ACTION

Crises are not always caused by acts of God; sometimes they are the deliberate acts of man, as with So Good soya milk in Australia. They received an anonymous threat that their drinks had been deliberately contaminated. Within six hours they had taken 300,000 packs off the shelves and destroyed them. Further to this, So Good established an emergency response team which had as one of its goals open communication, which was felt to be essential to win back consumer trust. It was agreed that all stages of the recall should be communicated to consumers, using every means available, so they would know exactly what was happening and when it was happening. The overriding theme was that every message had to reflect the fact that consumer safety was the company's number-one concern.

Changing the message was not a haphazard affair, as quantitative tracking research was conducted on a weekly basis to gauge when consumers had absorbed information to the extent that So Good could move on to the next stage of the message. They were also careful to avoid another knee-jerk reaction, that of deep price cuts. This was based on the belief that such action would have affected consumer perceptions by giving grounds for them believing there was something wrong with the product.

Such attention to detail paid off. The initial shock of the crisis had resulted in a drop of 381,000 litres in average weekly sales, of which it was estimated 226,000 had gone to competitors. Only eight weeks after the recall ended, however, So Good sales had already returned to their pre-recall levels, and three months after, its share was 2% above this level. Such increases reflected on the whole chilled soya category; within four and a half months its market share had gone from around 33% to 37% – the highest ever.

WHEN COWS AND BABIES NO LONGER MIXED

The threat to So Good had come from those with evil intent; in the UK the threat to regular milk came from those with the best of intentions: doctors and health visitors. They revised upwards the age at which they felt it was appropriate to give cow's milk to babies and stated that no cow's milk should be drunk by children under one year old. For the competition, in the form of formula milk manufacturers, it was Christmas. They went on the offensive, and mothers were left wondering whether there might be something fundamentally wrong with cow's milk.

"For the competition, in the form of formula milk manufacturers, it was Christmas"

Those marketing milk had to ensure there wasn't this sort of spillage in perceptions, as children aged one to five were a key market; indeed, they drank a third of all milk consumed, and milk accounted for 25% of their daily intake as opposed to only 2% for adults. To hold the fort, milk adopted the high ground of its calcium content. This was a key benefit, as milk is one of the richest sources of calcium, which helps kids' bones grow and aids children in growing big and strong. As such it symbolized the bond between a mother and her child – one of the strongest emotional cords. And this tug on the heartstrings pulled up consumption with the total number of servings of milk to the 0–5 age group rising by 14.67%. This was at a time when the number of children in this age group had fallen, which meant that the volume per capita consumption had increased by 15.6%.

The cases cited above registered high on the Richter scale of crisis. With Air New Zealand the level was low but no less real. It was going through a particularly bad time. It had suffered from the repercussions of the 9/11 bombings, but added to this had been the dramatic collapse of the Ansett Australia airline, coupled with increased vulnerability to low-cost competitors. A practical response was to adopt a low-fare strategy with the introduction of Express Class, which provided easier and cheaper online booking.

Prices alone were not enough, however; they needed to stimulate demand by giving reasons to travel, as 66% of the travelling public had never flown before. They wanted to reflect the reality of why people travel and to own the end-benefit they derive from it, rather than discussing aspects of the airline or the in-flight experience. This led to the proposition "being there is everything".

Such a multifaceted approach produced many positive results. Online bookings rose from 4% to 35% and, in the six months following the introduction of Express Class, passenger growth rose 21%. They also managed to extend the market with the percentage of first-time flyers rising from 4% to 9% and, although the objective had been to preserve the profitable corporate market, it actually grew by 9%. All this was in the face of Air New Zealand's domination of the market with a 66% share, which had been viewed as restricting any further growth, yet they managed to achieve a further 8% share. From a strictly business viewpoint, load factors increased from 70% to over 80%, and in the first six months the previous year's $350 million loss was turned into a $93 million half-year profit.

OVERALL

Strategy is above all an expression of clear thinking, and at no time is this at more of a premium than in a crisis. It is also the time when an awareness of the reaction of consumers and what can be done to assuage any negatives is vital.

Jack in the Box and So Good both took clear decisive action, and the pay-off was a position that eventually turned out to be better than they had enjoyed before the crisis.

Above all, these cases show that, however grave the crisis, it does not need to have a terminal effect on the brand. In some cases it can build on adversity – it serves to temper the brand's steel.

APPENDIX: INDEX OF BRAND CASE HISTORIES

SOURCES

AFA (Advertising Federation of Australia) Advertising Effectiveness Awards

CAANZ (The Communications Agencies Association of New Zealand) Effectiveness Awards

ICA (Institute of Communications and Advertising – Canada) CASSIE award-winners

IPA (Institute of Practitioners in Advertising) Effectiveness Awards, biennial book entitled *Advertising Works*

New York American Marketing Association Effie awards

With thanks to Matthew Coombs of the World Advertising Research Council (WARC) for his initial help and support.

ABOUT THE AUTHOR

Jonathan Cahill studied at the Sorbonne in Paris and in Heidelberg, as well as taking a degree in Economics and Politics at Newcastle University. He had a brief period greasing pumps in New Jersey and being a waiter in Atlanta. Subsequently he worked for many years in some of the largest international advertising agencies, such as Saatchi & Saatchi, Young & Rubicam, JWT and McCann Erickson, both in the UK and in Italy, where he was in charge of the advertising for Procter & Gamble's largest detergent brand in Europe. He worked on many well-known campaigns, helping to originate the "I bought the company" campaign for Remington shavers, which was used worldwide, and also formulating a strategy (for Rowntree's Fruit Pastilles) that is still in use 30 years later. Further to this he worked in a planning/research capacity with consultancies such as the Planning Partnership, the first independent planning consultancy.

In addition to this experience he has marketed several products of his own, including the Flexo lamp from Spain, which was seen there as prosaic and cheap, but whose position, through the invention of a brand and finely tuned marketing, he totally transformed in the UK. It became a best-seller in most of the leading design stores and the *Sunday Times* described it as "a masterpiece of modern design".

He continues to provide consultancy through his company Spring and to market products both in the UK and abroad.

Also published by Marshall Cavendish

THE VIKING MANIFESTO
The Scandinavian Approach to Business and Blasphemy
Steve Strid & Claes Andréasson

"Highly recommended. *The Viking Manifesto* makes for an interesting read and may prove a source of inspiration. Its advice is not so much practical and detailed – it is more about getting the spirit of entrepreneurship right and growing your brand in line with the Scandinavian way."

Start Your Business

The Vikings used to drink from the skulls of their enemies. Now they sell furniture in flat boxes.

They took a civilization based on pillaging, plundering and narcotic mushrooms and gave us the Nobel Prize, IKEA, Ericsson, Lego and Absolut. With a population of just under 20 million for Sweden, Denmark, Norway and Iceland, today's Vikings only account for 0.3 per cent of the world's population, yet produce a whopping 3 per cent of all world exports. Scandinavian products are first-rate, but it is their brands that have swept the world.

The violence is gone, but modern Vikings still have an ingenious and slightly blasphemous approach to making a name for their companies, products and causes. *The Viking Manifesto* explains why advertising doesn't work and why this is good, why competition is nonsense, why reward and punishment are an inferior form of motivation, and why money doesn't make the world go round. It's method without the madness. It's old, it's new and it works.

The Vikings are back and this time they mean business.

ISBN 978-0-462-09932-3 / £7.99 Paperback

Also published by Marshall Cavendish

THE INVISIBLE GRAIL
How Brands Can Use Words to Engage with Audiences
John Simmons

"How to make love, not war, with words. The Invisible Grail
is absolutely chock full of insight and fresh ideas about
brands, business and language."

James Hill, former Chairman, Birds Eye Wall's

All brands want to be loved. Creating that positive emotional
connection between product and audience is brand management's
holy grail. But not all brands achieve this goal. And perhaps the
ones that most want to be loved are the ones that fall short of
finding affection. What are these brands missing? How can they
bring themselves closer to their customers and their own people?
How can they reveal the grail?

The Invisible Grail argues that the secret to unearthing this
ultimate prize already exists within most businesses. But it lies
hidden. Beaten down by the continued over-emphasis on visual
impact. The answer lies within the power of the brand's verbal
identity – the words and stories that are used to represent what
the brand stands for.

What is verbal identity? And where can it be found, lurking,
hidden from view? *The Invisible Grail* answers those questions by
taking the reader on a quest that explores the extraordinary but
neglected power of language to bring brands and their audiences
into more rewarding relationships.

The Invisible Grail is an immensely stimulating book for anyone
close to brands. It will take you on a captivating journey of
discovery with a valuable treasure awaiting at the end.

ISBN 978-1-904879-69-5 / £9.99 Paperback

Also published by Marshall Cavendish

ONE

A Consumer Revolution for Business

Stefan Engeseth

"Some people believe you need to think outside of the box. That's silly. What you need is a much bigger box. Stefan Engeseth will help you find one."

Seth Godin, marketing guru and author of *Purple Cow*

The power of the consumer is greater than it has ever been. Yet the gap between what companies promise and what consumers experience has never been wider. If companies are to survive and thrive in this age of the consumer, they need to interact with their customers. They need to let customers into their processes for creating new products and services, and even into their marketing and selling.

Most big companies still run their business as a monologue. Though they may try to talk to customers on a one-to-one basis, they aren't really listening. But in a time of ad-skipping, blogs, hate websites and consumer activism, they can't afford to stay so aloof. Brands are powerful only when they are relevant to consumers – when companies take what's important to the target audience and make it an integral part of the brand. For that to happen, brand and consumers must work together as one.

Drawing on a wealth of anecdotes, examples and cutting-edge ideas, this revolutionary new book offers methods, tools and inspiration to bring customers closer to your company. *ONE* is nothing less than a new marketing manifesto. Read it and learn how to make consumer power work for your company, not against it.

ISBN 978-0-462-09941-5 / £9.99 Paperback

Also published by Marshall Cavendish

SEE, FEEL, THINK, DO
The Power of Instinct in Business
Andy Milligan & Shaun Smith

"This book gives you the inspiration and confidence to follow your gut."

Charles Dunstone, CEO, The Carphone Warehouse

See, Feel, Think, Do: The power of instinct in business describes a simple, yet powerful, technique that lies behind some of the best inventions and most innovative product and service ideas in business today. Put simply, it is the idea that by watching and empathizing with real customers and how they act, we can develop ideas that solve their real needs.

For a while it looked as if MBA models, focus groups and CRM systems were in danger of taking over from good old human instinct and a passion for making a difference. Now we are seeing that many of the best and most innovative business ideas are coming from business leaders who operate more from their own gut instinct and insight rather than endless analysis.

Tim Waterstone started his chain of bookstores using just this approach. Philip Green has tripled earnings of the Arcadia Group with his hands-on style. David Neeleman, founder of US airline JetBlue Airways, used these principles to propel his airline from a start-up in 1999 to a US$1-billion company today. It has produced the Apple iPod, led to drive-through check-ins and low-cost flights; it has affected the ways that Heinz market ketchup and NASA teach their astronauts safety.

The authors draw on examples from many of the world's most successful entrepreneurs, from people as diverse as Steve Jobs, Gordon Ramsay, George Soros, Richard Branson and Jeff Bezos to organizations as varied as Tesco, EMC², Progressive, Clifford Chance, TNT and Geek Squad.

See, Feel, Think, Do is a thought-provoking and highly practical book that shows how the power of instinct can transform your business.

ISBN 978-1-905736-25-6 / £9.99 Paperback